# VALUES
OVER
# VALUABLES

# VALUES
## OVER
# VALUABLES

### DARING TO LIVE THE LIFE
### MONEY CAN'T BUY

## HARMON KONG

**Forbes** | Books

Published by Forbes Books, Charleston, South Carolina.
An imprint of Advantage Media Group.

Forbes Books is a registered trademark, and the Forbes Books colophon is a trademark of Forbes Media, LLC.

Printed in the United States of America.

10  9  8  7  6  5  4  3  2  1

ISBN: 979-8-88750-219-9 (Hardcover)
ISBN: 979-8-88750-220-5 (eBook)

Library of Congress Control Number: 2024912627

Cover and layout design by Matthew Morse.

Since 1917, Forbes has remained steadfast in its mission to serve as the defining voice of entrepreneurial capitalism. Forbes Books, launched in 2016 through a partnership with Advantage Media, furthers that aim by helping business and thought leaders bring their stories, passion, and knowledge to the forefront in custom books. Opinions expressed by Forbes Books authors are their own. To be considered for publication, please visit **books.Forbes.com**.

*To all those who have chosen to read this book
and embark on this journey.*

*May these pages provide you with inspiration,
encouragement, and guidance, helping you and your family
live lives of enduring significance beyond mere success,
creating a lasting impact for generations.*

# Contents

Acknowledgments

-1-

A Word from the Author

-3-

INTRODUCTION

The Best Investment

-5-

CHAPTER 1

Doing Well by Doing Good

-15-

CHAPTER 2

How Much Is Enough?

-35-

CHAPTER 3

## The Price of Everything and the Value of Nothing

-55-

CHAPTER 4

## Redefining Financial Freedom

-75-

CHAPTER 5

## Significance Beyond Success

-89-

CHAPTER 6

## Living Is Giving

-107-

CHAPTER 7

## Everyone Is Included

-119-

CONCLUSION

## The Power of Teamwork

-131-

FROM THE AUTHOR

## Thank You for Reading
*Values Over Valuables*

-137-

APPENDIX A

## Discovering My Values Worksheet

-139-

APPENDIX B

## Sample Family Vision and Mission Statements

-145-

APPENDIX C

## Family Goal Sheet

-151-

APPENDIX D

## Kong Ohana House Rules

-155-

# ACKNOWLEDGMENTS

First, I give all the glory to God. Each day is a tapestry of blessings, woven with threads of grace. This book stands as a testament to His faithfulness and divine guidance.

My heartfelt thanks go to my amazing, faithful wife, Lea, your grace in my shortcomings and constant inspiration have driven me to be a better husband.

To my four children, Tyler, Haley, Troy, and Kyle, I am deeply grateful for your unwavering support and unconditional love. Being your dad is by far my greatest honor and achievement. I am so proud of each of you!

To my parents, Mom, who is no longer with us, you were my greatest fan growing up; your belief in me has always been a source of strength. You taught me that being a family is so much more than just having a family. Dad, your legacy of faith, hard work, and generosity is something I will always strive to emulate. Thank you for instilling these values in me.

To my Apriem family, your collaborative spirit has helped shape a company that truly values people and relationships, a true reflection of our shared vision. I am proud of what we have accomplished together. I am thankful for my loyal partners and leadership team, Rhonda, Ben,

Landon, Shawn, Jennifer, and Christopher, who continue to strive to be our best for those we serve. Teamwork makes a dream work!

To our cherished Apriem clients, I want to personally thank you for trusting us to steward your family finances. Your loyalty and partnership have been the cornerstone of our success. It's an honor to serve you and your family, and we are committed to continually exceeding your expectations.

To my incredible community of friends, thank you for the shared laughter and tears. Your presence in my life adds depth and meaning to every experience. Your friendship is a treasure.

Finally, a special thanks to everyone at Forbes Books who worked on this book project. I would not have been able to complete it without your expertise and patience throughout this entire journey. I am especially grateful to Nate Best, who spent countless hours ensuring this book became a reality. Your dedication and encouragement have been instrumental in bringing this project to fruition. You are the best!

# A WORD FROM THE AUTHOR

————————

*My tastes are simple. I simply like the best.* That was the slogan on a poster that my good friend Sam taped on the wall in high school and in his dorm room during his time at USC undergraduate and UCLA graduate college days. Those words became sort of his mantra for success. Today, he runs a private equity firm that manages a couple billion dollars.

Through the years, as Sam and I pursued our careers in wealth management, we each moved beyond a focus on material things. In the world of money and markets, as we helped our clients grow their fortunes, we saw clearly how financial wealth alone does not make people's lives simpler. It often adds layers of complication and relational stress.

Today, we recognize that "best" means something more: We simply like what matters most. Values matter more than valuables. People matter more than profits.

That perspective grew as Sam and I discovered that we shared a passion for matters of faith. We had spent years studying the financial markets and learning how to build wealth—and we had established that we were good at it. As we studied Scripture, however, we saw, as King Solomon declared, that there is nothing new under the sun.

Many concepts that govern good money management were written thousands of years ago.

The Bible has more than 2,000 references to money and possessions. That's more mentions than love, peace, and forgiveness combined. Many people misquote Scripture to say that money is the root of all evil. Not so. It's the *love* of money that leads us astray. Instead, we should love its power to bring meaning into our lives. It should serve a purpose. If you love money, you are more likely to use others to gain it rather than use money to show love to others. I believe this is why families are expected to grow their resources and steward their money wisely.

*Live simply so others can simply live* has become the new slogan in life for Sam and his family.

You don't need to have a PhD in finance or accounting to successfully manage your finances. To do well, you will need to define and follow a solid set of principles. What are your life's guiding principles?

Faith is paramount in my family. Though I will not sermonize in the pages ahead, I do want to be clear at the outset about what drives me personally and professionally.

In this book, I will share the prescription for fiscal fitness as I have come to understand it. In doing so, I wish to gently reflect the faith that, in my family, comes first. God wants his people to love him—with all our heart, soul, and mind—and he wants us to love our neighbors as we love ourselves. All else flows from that beautiful simplicity. All other values arise from that purity of purpose.

While the tales and descriptions featured in this book are true recollections, details and personal information have been changed to respect and uphold the privacy of individuals and entities.

# The Best Investment

---

*Ohana* was the heartbeat of how I grew up. In Hawaiian culture, the word means family in the embracing sense of community—a people who stand united, sharing joys and sorrow. To treat others like family is the spirit that shaped my outlook on life, and it has shaped how I do business today.

I was not born in Hawaii as my parents were; both of them grew up in small towns on the island of Oahu. When I was a boy, we often visited my grandparents and other relatives in Hawaii, which we still considered home. On weekends, we would all go to the park to barbecue, swim, fish, and celebrate our time together. To get a good picnic spot at the Ala Moana or Queen Kapiolani park, we needed to arrive early. Those weekend family gatherings are a long-standing tradition for many local Hawaiian islanders.

The spirit of *ohana* hit home for me at one such outing, when I was about five years old. I recall that day vividly—the music of laughter, the shouts of children splashing along the shore, the sizzling of the barbecues. I held my dad's hand as we strolled over to a group of men and women nearby who stood chatting and gazing over the surf. His words to them were warm and inviting as he gestured toward our table: "Eh, you folks like join us. We going kakou soon." My parents often spoke English with a Hawaiian pidgin accent, so the message translates to, "I hope you can join us. We'll be sitting to eat soon." They smiled but politely declined, patting their bellies to say they were already full.

"Dad? Who were those people?" I asked him a few minutes later as he tended to the short ribs, his specialty, on the barbecue while my mom mixed her amazing potato salad.

"Just some folks like us enjoying the beautiful day at the park."

"So they're not our relatives like my aunties and uncles?"

My father knelt and looked into my eyes, smiling tenderly. "Yes, Harmon," he said. "They are." And that is when he explained to me something beautiful and profound that became a guiding value in my life.

During my school days in northern California, where my dad pursued his career as a professor of life sciences, I observed that not everyone shared our values. I saw some families that were torn from within by strife.

In my profession as a wealth manager and a financial advisor, I have witnessed such family dysfunction many times since. I have mediated meetings between bitter brothers who refused to speak to each other over some seemingly trivial matter. I have seen tears of regret over relationships lost. I have seen families fragmented—and, very often, money is at the root of the discord.

It is all so unnecessary. Used wisely, money can work wonders. It can be a force for great good instead of the harm that it so often inflicts on families and society. When people are willing to talk openly and listen from the heart, they can find unity and understanding, even when their views still differ. The right perspective is what makes the difference—and that is the spirit that I discovered so long ago at my father's side during our weekend barbecues at the beach parks.

## Time to Talk

Within the next few decades, the baby boomers among us will be passing on trillions of dollars to the next generations. That's a staggering amount and a staggering responsibility. The importance of doing this well cannot be overstated, given the potential ramifications.

By and large, today's financial industry has been sending the wrong message to the boomers and their babies. The industry tends to focus not on people but on the bottom line. On Wall Street, some of the financial players measure progress strictly by gain, stripping money of any real purpose other than propagating itself. They encourage the love of money, for its own sake, more than the power of money to "spread da Aloha," or love, as they say in the islands.

As a result, many of the people who come to me for financial advice have been under the impression that money can solve all their problems. Their primary concern, at the outset, is how they can generate more and more wealth to take care of various family issues. If they could just make a lot more money, everything would be all right—*right*?

It doesn't work that way. No amount of money can fix a family when the fundamentals are failing. Such dysfunction can lead to everyone suing everyone—children fighting parents, sibling fighting sibling. The money only adds fuel to the fire, and it all just goes up in a brighter blaze.

As a man who makes his living by managing money for others, I try to help people to get back on track. What I tell them is the same message that I emphasize throughout these chapters: One's values are more important than the value of one's portfolio. Don't get me wrong: I pay close attention to both. Money matters immensely; it's just that *you* matter more.

To those who seek my advice, I often ask questions such as these: *Would leaving more money to your kids be better for them? Would you rather they live on what they earn or what they inherit? Should they work hard for their money, or should their money work hard for them? If you turned out fine without anyone leaving a fortune to you, why would you feel compelled to leave a fortune to your kids?*

There's no right or wrong response. You can make a case either way. Leaving money to loved ones is an honorable gesture. I just want my clients to start considering carefully whether what they are doing, or how they do it, is in everyone's best interest and makes the most sense in the long run. Have they ever paused to ask why?

I have met many family leaders who are re-examining their priorities. After years in the swirl, they are wondering what it's all about. They are not so sure anymore that inheriting money will improve the lives of their children. Weary of the race, they cut to the chase: *Should we just keep accumulating more and more wealth? Isn't there a legacy that is greater than money?* Nothing is wrong with the desire to prosper, but at some level of wealth, money loses its utility, meaning more of it does not add to the quantity or quality of one's life.

In many families, sadly, so much is left unsaid. Money can become such a touchy subject that people hesitate to speak about it, even with closest loved ones, for fear of hurting feelings or arousing anger. But what goes unspoken can cause hurt and anger, too. Misunderstandings can breed resentments that fester into feuds.

It's time to talk. It's time that families engaged in a conversation that is not a tweet, a text, or a social media post—a real discussion about what matters most. That is what it takes to promote unity, peace, and understanding. That is how families can rediscover and reinforce the principles that produced their prosperity.

# The Apriem Way

For three decades, since I was in my early twenties and fresh out of college, I have worked with hundreds of families on their financial affairs, helping them to make the most of their money to accomplish their goals and dreams. In thousands of conversations through the years, I have heard just about every angle of what families go through as they try to manage their finances and lives.

The founding of Apriem Advisors in 1998 was inspired out of frustration over my earlier experiences in the financial industry. Over the years, my initial enthusiasm had faded as I observed how often money had much to do with messing up people's lives. Not only can it worsen dysfunction, it can cause it. I encountered people who felt driven to make a bundle without a sense of purpose. They never stopped to ask why. It became increasingly clear to me that a lot of advisors in the industry weren't asking why, either. They were more interested in chasing dollars for themselves and pursuing larger accounts, desiring to work with corporations, pension plans, and multimillion-dollar portfolios.

That wasn't for me. I wanted to help individuals and families secure their financial future while achieving peace of mind by making wise decisions about their finances. I wanted a deeper understanding of how their beliefs about money influence those decisions and affect the people in their lives. I knew this was a critical step toward their financial freedom.

To do business the way I wanted, I resolved to launch my own independent practice focusing on families and their overall well-being. I knew that developing meaningful relationships should not be optional. It should be everything. Our perspective ever since has been *less is more*, meaning that having fewer clients lets us provide greater service. As a reminder of why we do what we do, my company president gave me a ceramic tile with those words on it.

In addition, we resolved to serve our clients "to the highest degree"—which is the Latin-based meaning of *Apriem*. We would do so by working with them one-on-one, emphasizing the importance of giving purpose to their money and instilling their values in the next generation. That would be our mission. That would be the Apriem Way.

As I write this, Apriem has developed into a boutique multigenerational wealth management firm with over a billion dollars in assets under management and growing clients in almost every state. We are registered investment advisors with the Securities and Exchange Commission, and as such, we have a fiduciary obligation to serve our clients' best interests. We do not engage in the typical broker relationship where products are bought and sold to investors for commission or additional compensation. Sadly, many investors do not know how their advisor gets compensated. Apriem manages client investment portfolios, through the Charles Schwab Corp., but we are not ourselves an investment banker or brokers. Our foremost focus is on overall family financial planning. That must come first. We need to know the *why* before recommending the *how*.

While two families might appear comparable in terms of balance sheets, cash flow, and tax situations, they can be vastly different. Each family possesses a distinct financial DNA, with its own financial history and dynamics. As fiduciaries, our goal is to provide recommendations and advice that prioritize our clients' well-being above all else.

# Why I Wrote This Book

As the cofounder and chief wealth manager of Apriem, I work primarily with relatively affluent folks who are financially comfortable yet are looking to grow in other ways. Often, they are questioning the deeper meaning of their life's work and considering how they will give back from their good fortunes. They are interested in doing better—financially, of course, but not strictly in terms of dollars. Though such wealthy families make up much of the clientele of our firm, we do offer services to people who have more modest portfolios. All will find this book to be insightful as they reflect on their decision-making.

The advice here will be helpful to heads of household of any financial caliber. Your cup may be full, overflowing, or still filling up. You might be at the beginning or end of your career. You might be a veteran of financial affairs, or perhaps you are just starting out with only a 401(k) or IRA. Maybe you are a newly widowed mother with grown children and a dearth of knowledge about how to handle the family wealth that is now in your control. You could be a parent wondering which of your children, if any, will be ready and able to steward the family business and financial assets. You may decide to give this book to the young adults in your household to help them set out on a solid footing. Or you and your spouse could read it together as you strive toward family unity and marital solidarity.

You will find no shortage of authors and columnists and talking heads out there who don't know you but nonetheless are eager to offer their take on what you should do with your money. What's best for your neighbor or coworker may not at all be what is best for you—and investment tips and strategies that serve you well one year often become unwise for you the next. My team and I have years of experience that qualifies us to give you the regular, individual attention that you need to truly succeed. We don't simply plug you into an algorithm. We plug into your life.

My goal in writing this book is to distill the complicated world of finances into the themes that will make the biggest difference for families like yours. I did not set out to write something that reads like an MBA textbook on how to get rich fast. Instead, you will find stories of real people making their way in the world, sometimes winning, sometimes losing, trying to do what's right for themselves, their families, and posterity. My aim is to offer advice that is evergreen. I want your grandchildren, when they venture out into the world, to find this book as relevant as the day it was published.

The common denominator among those who will benefit from this book is the desire to do what's best for the people in their lives. They want to devise a wealth and retirement plan that will serve them well—and perhaps outlive them to help their families and a world of many needs. You will find guidance on the kind of candid communication in which every family should engage before it's too late. We will look at the fundamentals and the fine points of those family conversations.

If you are hungry for honest, friendly, helpful guidance, read on. You will rediscover what matters most. The content of your character is your greatest asset. It's not about bigger accounts, friends. It's about a bigger life.

# The Greatest Investment

Every family leader has a responsibility to steward resources wisely, and that means passing on wisdom along with the wealth to the next generation. It also means sharing and passing down values more so than your valuables. Ideally, the goal should be financial freedom, which is something different to everyone. This we know: It doesn't always mean more money. The pot of gold is an elusive prize, and the quest to stake the biggest claim can leave a family splintered. When the underpinnings of family values are secure, more money can open wondrous opportunities. It can promote freedom and unity. But without those strong values, money can breed mayhem.

In my years as an advisor, I have seen people come to tears in my office as we talk about their forgotten dreams and damaged relationships. I have seen outbursts of anger and eye rolls of disdain among people who pledged their lives to each other and should be holding hands in unity.

What's the best investment today? I'm often asked that question, and I could talk for hours about securities and asset classes and sectors and such. I know in my heart, though, that the best investment has been the same for all time, and it's either pay now or pay later. You get the greatest dividends and the healthiest return by investing in the people in your life. When you give your relationships priority over your portfolio, you have a reliable growth strategy. When you put family first, you have something money can't buy. You have *ohana*.

# CHAPTER 1

# Doing Well by Doing Good

Richard was a wealthy businessman, with a net worth in the multi-millions—that is, if the worth of a human being can be distilled into dollars. He was not feeling particularly rich, though, as we sat over lunch one day.

As so often happens whenever I talk with clients, our discussion eventually turned from finances to family. Richard and I had been working together for several years. He was in his sixties, at the peak of a stellar career. I was a young guy not far into my thirties, hungry for success. My wife, Lea, and I still felt like newlyweds—though we already had two small children, with a set of twins on the way.

I filled him in, proudly, on the latest details of our family life and shared some photos. Richard hadn't said a word for a few minutes, though he seemed to be listening intently. He picked up a saltshaker, studied it a moment, and then looked straight into my face. His eyes were wet.

"You know my daughter Sophia's getting married this June," he said, struggling to keep his composure.

Uncertain whether these were tears of joy or anguish, I tried to think of the right thing to say. "That's awesome. And I'm sure you'll be giving her a fine wedding."

"Yeah. She'll get the wedding of her dreams. And I could give her ten weddings like that. I sure do have the money." He gazed out the window. "What I don't have is *her*."

"What's going on, Richard?" I asked. I knew that this was no time to offer advice, or to suggest solutions, or to say much at all. What this man needed me to do now was listen.

"We haven't been getting along," he said. "I don't have much of a role in Sophia's wedding, or the planning of it. My job is to pay for it all, she tells me. That's what I get to do. Foot the bill. I suppose it's okay with her if I show up the day of the wedding."

He paused. "Harmon, don't make the same mistake I did."

"What do you mean?"

"That family of yours, those two beautiful little kids. That's what makes you a wealthy man. Not all the money in the world."

My thoughts turned to Tyler and Haley, probably just settling down for an afternoon nap. I wondered whether I'd be home in time to kiss them good night.

"You know, I always thought I was doing the right thing," Richard continued. "I was going to be the great provider so my family would want for nothing. I knew how to make money. And I was *good* at it." He was, indeed. We had just finished reviewing his investments and fine-tuning his portfolio, and his family certainly was well-set.

I nodded. "Yes, you've done well." I don't think that's quite what he wanted to hear at the moment.

"Not all *that* well," he said, sharply. "My relationship was with the almighty dollar, with material things. Not with her. I wasn't there for her, and she knew it. I was just so … so *busy* all the time. So busy doing right by my family. Or that's what I told myself."

Richard's words came haltingly as he tried not to sob. "She's my baby girl," he said, tapping his forefinger on the table. "I always thought I'd be walking her down the aisle someday. Seems now she doesn't want me around much at all."

I never have forgotten that scene, or Richard's advice to me: *Don't make the same mistake.…* Those words echoed in my head as I walked back to my office to crunch more numbers and cultivate more clients. I knew that I was helping them to make money, and I, like Richard, found it challenging and fun. I enjoyed finances. I still do. I have found it gratifying to see how smart investments can help families attain their goals. Still, my gut felt uneasy as I left the restaurant that day.

Richard was telling me that he had discovered, too late, that there are smarter types of investments than just the ones on Wall Street, and that there are loftier goals than beating some benchmark. I think that as he looked at me that day, he saw something of himself as a younger man brimming with ambition to do his utmost for his wife and child. He shared his pain and regrets with me not out of self-pity but as a warning, man to man, that came down to this: *Get your priorities straight, friend—because if you don't, all this talk about investments won't count for beans.*

Thank you, Richard.

# "Why" before "How"

In working with families, the financial industry tends to do things backward. The conventional approach to wealth management focuses on the *how* rather than the *why*. How can you make more money, reduce your taxes, and grow a bigger and bigger portfolio? There's not much emphasis on what you are growing and its purpose. Growth for its own sake makes little sense. A farmer could cultivate a bumper crop of ragweed, but why? The harvest would be plentiful but pointless.

In the two decades since my talk with Richard, I have encountered many families that have failed to master the meaning of money. I see parents spending boatloads of dollars, for example, to send their children to expensive, prestigious schools, believing that's the ticket to a lucrative career, only to find that the kids don't care about law or medicine or engineering and would prefer to study something that interests them. Parents understandably want a good return on their college investment, but young people have their own ideas and don't necessarily buy into the notion that money buys happiness.

A practical man, my father urged me while I was still in high school to look for a solid career that would earn me a comfortable living. I did all right in school, though I wasn't a straight-A student like my older brother. I was into sports. I ran track as a sprinter, and I played football until all my teammates got bigger than me. As often as I could, I hit the slopes, and skiing is still a favorite pastime. My high school years were less about academics and more about making friends. I enjoyed learning about people. My dad saw me as a smart kid who needed to be pointed in the right direction. One evening, he knocked on my bedroom door and asked to talk. "You've got to start thinking about college," he said.

I decided to play with his head. "*Why?*" I asked, as if the thought never had occurred to me.

"Well, because once you get a degree, nobody can ever take that away from you no matter what."

"A degree? Why do I need one of those?"

"It will help you get a good job, Harmon."

I wasn't about to stop. "Why do I need a job?"

Dad looked at the ceiling, then deep into my eyes. He had often told us kids that there are no stupid questions, but he just might have doubted his conviction right about then. "You need a job," he said slowly, "so you can make a decent living, because you aren't going to be living here forever, son. You're going to get out there and support yourself."

And he meant it. Like most teenagers in those days, I looked forward to getting a car when I turned sixteen so I could be free at last. That's fine, he told me, so long as I earned the money to buy it, and the gas, and the insurance, too. So, I did. I gave up sports and started working at a retail nursery, the perfect gig for the son of a horticulture enthusiast. It was a natural fit for me. That job got me my car—and in the years to come, it helped get me through college.

As it turned out, my father didn't need to worry that I might pursue a higher education in basket weaving. I had a natural interest in finances. I read *Money* magazine when I was in high school and would ask my dad questions like: "So, hey, you're a smart guy, are you watching the tech stocks?" or "Check out these mutual funds, wow, do you even know about these, Dad?" I kept jabbing at him, for no particular reason, until one day he said, "You know what, son? When you go out and make your fortune you can do what you want with your money, but until then I'll do what I think is best with my money." He wasn't about to listen to a seventeen-year-old money manager.

As I examined the "why" of a higher education, that early interest in finances persisted. I wanted to be a good steward of the modest resources that I had and to make the most of whatever better might come my way. A financial career would be a good fit for me. As I envisioned it, I could make a decent living while also learning about people and helping them to better themselves in meaningful ways. I would not be pursuing wealth for its own sake. I had a purpose to fulfill. I would do well by doing good.

And several years into my career, my dad decided he *could* listen to a twenty-five-year-old money manager and let me handle his retirement funds. "Just remember," he said with a smile, "if you mess this up, I'm going to come to live with you for the rest of my life"—and, smiling back at him, I assured him that no way on earth would I let that happen.

It took me a while, though, to find my groove. In my early career, when I met Richard and others like him, I was seeing more and more how money can become a curse while masquerading as a blessing. I saw people who were fabulously successful, by worldly standards, yet so in thrall to the power of money that they had forgotten why they were making it.

These were not bad people. They wanted to do well, by and large, but were merely misguided. Or at least lost in the pursuit of wealth at all costs even if it damaged their marriage or their family. They adhered to the conventional wisdom of the wealth management industry that separates your financial life from the rest of your life. In doing so, they lost perspective. They no longer could see what mattered most—their loved ones who wanted more of their time, not less. Money was supposed to give them that. Instead, it robbed them of it.

When I finally said my farewell to my corporate career at Fidelity Investments after almost nine years, I was determined to refocus on families to help them truly get the most out of their money, primarily by imbuing their money with meaning. It was at the family level that I felt that I could make the biggest difference. I wanted to work with folks who were building and growing toward something better but perhaps wondering what that might be. I wanted to work with people who felt that a sizable income alone didn't mean they were "doing well."

At Fidelity, I had to work with close to five hundred households, and to do that effectively was next to impossible. I felt as if I was racing to put out fires every day, working sixty-hour weeks, and the company expected me to bring in additional clients beyond those already on my roster. After all, I had been brought in to build the clientele. I was inundated and frustrated. Life would be so different, I thought, if I could just focus on a tenth as many clients—say, fifty families—and without a corporate agenda tying my hands.

Since our founding, Apriem Advisors has taken a holistic view of wealth, helping families to find balance in their lives. I was determined that everyone who joined our firm would be able to put a priority on family life. We rejected a growth-at-all-costs mentality. We were content to give ourselves the flexibility to go home at a reasonable time and to attend our children's activities rather than stay late at the office.

My founding partner, who since has gone on to other pursuits, likewise came from a corporate background in a bank trust department, where he, like me, recognized what he didn't want to be doing for the rest of his career. He, too, recently had started a family, and we both realized that this was a special and fleeting time in our lives. Our top priority was to our loved ones, as husband and father.

With our "less is more" philosophy, we resolved to serve fewer clients far better. We dedicated ourselves to helping families, but we never forgot that we had our own families—and that is the culture that continues to this day at Apriem. Our litmus test for how well we serve each client is this: Are we giving that person the same quality of advice that we would give our parents and grandparents, our brothers and sisters, our aunts and uncles? Are we treating that person like family? Would we hire ourselves?

We help people manage their money wisely while remembering the adage that money isn't everything. Having a lot of it doesn't mean you will prosper. We help families grow their wealth, certainly, but along the way we also offer a wealth of wisdom. We offer the prospect of prosperity with perspective.

Our culture had much to do with our current company president's decision to join us. Rhonda had been working sixty-hour weeks in a corporate position at a Wall Street-based firm. "What I have to offer you," I told her, "is a job where you will never miss your sons' baseball games—and you'll be there for the whole game, not just the end of the ninth inning." She was delighted to join our operation, a much smaller one than she had known but dedicated to solid values.

Much of today's financial industry misses most of the ball game. It measures prosperity by the size of a portfolio. I have devoted decades to helping others make the most of their assets—which means money, for sure, but more. A well-planned portfolio can redefine what is possible in a well-planned life. Wealth gives you choices. It opens doors, but it's up to you to walk through them to find something of lasting significance. The best thing that money can buy is the time to do something besides making money. With that time, you can make memories. You can pursue a purpose. Will you invest in something that will outlive you?

"No other success can compensate for failure in the home," said James E. McCulloch nearly a hundred years ago in his book *Home: The Savior of Civilization.* That wisdom resonates today. It's a common scenario: Anticipating big financial rewards, professionals and entrepreneurs toil away for countless hours, telling themselves this will be only for a while, until they establish themselves and the cash rolls in, when they will cut back to just a few hours a day and devote themselves to family. A year turns to decades, and they are still on the treadmill, even when they long since could have jumped off.

Here's what happens: They get good at making money, and they want more of it. They begin to gain their sense of significance from the job, or the business, rather than their home life. Nothing wrong with making money—except when it becomes an addiction, a craving, a pursuit without purpose, and more importantly built on the back of families! Some things that feel good can kill you. What was supposed to become financial independence instead can become financial bondage. They have more financial security than needed yet no peace of mind.

Every family leader should ask a fundamental question: *On what foundation am I building my house?* It must be something more substantial than the digits on your financial statements. What is money but paper and cheap metal? You might collect a mountain of it just to find yourself buried under worry and stress. If money is your master, your goals will feel elusive, illusory, unattainable. That's because money is a means, not an end. Strong values are the foundation that endures. You need those strong values to stand up to life's storms, and your children need them, too. Their success depends more upon the transfer of those values rather than the amount of your valuables.

# Teaching the Children Well

My parents met in Hawaii when they were teenagers, and my dad was still in college when they married. Within several years, they had five kids, and my mother's full-time career was raising us. My two older brothers were born in Hawaii, and I was born in Oregon where Dad was finishing his graduate work. My younger brother and sister were born after we followed his career to northern California.

As a professor, my father was passionate about education and demonstrated that value. Intensely curious, he was fascinated with anything involving the life sciences: marine biology, botany, biology, oceanography, and chemistry, to name a few of his specialties. He preferred the intimate setting of a community college to the supersized culture of a major university. He wanted smaller classes and a closer connection to his students. Eventually, he became president of a local community college and finished his career as a college chancellor.

For most of my childhood, we lived in a rural region near Sacramento. Ours was the house where everyone wanted to hang out, it seemed, and it often bustled with visiting schoolmates, friends, and neighbors. We had only a two-acre lot, much smaller than the nearby farms, but we made the most of it. On half that land, my father raised steer and chickens which became our source of meat and eggs. On the other half, we had a vegetable garden, fruit trees, beehives, and greenhouses for the family bonsai business. My parents sold the bonsai trees wholesale and conducted classes on the art of pruning them. On many weekends, we also sold them at swap meets. To teach us the value of incentives, my dad paid my brothers and me a commission. I found that I could make a hundred dollars over a weekend—not bad for a seventh-grader.

A big household needs to economize, particularly when living on a professor's limited salary, so I wore a lot of hand-me-downs from my two older brothers. My younger brother got new stuff because after it got to me, I destroyed it, sparing him from having to wear a fourth round. We got used to hearing that we couldn't afford to buy things. Instead, we *did* things, as a family. In the summers, when my dad wasn't teaching, the family took long road trips and did a lot of camping. Along the way, Dad would give us impromptu nature lectures.

I can't say I was much interested in my father's observations on the flora and fauna. I just wanted to get where we were going and have fun. I know now that what he wanted was quality time with his family. He treasured memories more than material things. Our time spent together united us, and that family unity was a central value for him. My parents recognized that relationships matter most—and in my own family, we have followed their template of togetherness.

My father was an organic farmer before organic was popular. We grew soybeans, tomatoes, and corn and maintained a large compost pile for organic waste that would later be used as fertilizer. If my parents saw worms and insects in the garden, no way would we spray insecticide. Instead, our mom paid us a quarter for every worm we picked out of the tomato plants. Then, my dad figured out that if we peeled back the husk of each ear of corn slightly at the top and poured a little vegetable oil on the silk, the worms would stay away. I was recruited for that task, spending tedious hours in the garden with a T-shirt wrapped around my face to keep the corn blades from slicing me.

"*Why?*" I asked my dad one day as I emerged from the garden. "Why are we doing this? It's a waste of our time." I wiped my brow with the T-shirt. "They sell good corn at the grocery store. Plenty of tomatoes and peppers, too, and every cut of meat. Let's just buy what we need!"

My dad half-smiled as he looked at his surly son. Though he disagreed wholeheartedly, he clearly respected my independent thinking and my challenge to the status quo. "No, our own food is better," he simply said. This was the 1970s, at the dawn of the environmental movement. He had been hearing about the development of genetically altered seeds and the devastation from chemical pesticides and fertilizers. He and his botanist colleagues were becoming deeply concerned. That's why we grew a lot of our own food and raised steers and chickens.

As I look back, I know my dad was right. Our backyard sweet corn was near perfection, free of worms, and infinitely tastier than what came from the store. Dad knew what he was doing and why it was worth our time and effort. He demonstrated to us that he was a man true to his values. He kept his priorities straight and taught us to do the same, in whatever endeavor we chose in life. To this day, he still has many fruit trees in his yard and loves to share his crops with his friends and neighbors.

In a world of endless responsibilities, keeping priorities straight isn't all that easy. We can spend a lifetime scrambling to live up to what we think others expect of us. For generations, society has conditioned men to be the tireless breadwinners and leave the nurturing to the women. The message: *Get a job, support your family.* Even as family dynamics have shifted, old attitudes die hard. As women have risen to top leadership roles, they too face social biases, spoken or not. The message: *Go home, take care of your kids.* The simple truth is that children need parents who will fill both their material and emotional needs. It's about finding the right balance.

I have fallen short at times in striking that balance. No parent can walk that line perfectly. What matters is recognizing when you slip and making amends. I think back through the years to a bright and windy spring day when our four children were small and we had just purchased a new SUV, big enough to accommodate all six of us and the boundless variety of kid stuff. There it sat in our driveway, shining in the sun. As we were leaving on a family outing that morning, one of our boys opened the passenger door and a gust of wind caught it, slamming it into the side of our other car.

"No!" I hollered, as I rushed over to see substantial dings in both vehicles. Although he had done nothing more dreadful than open a door—did I expect him to control the wind?—I scolded him, leaving him crying and me feeling ridiculous. I am embarrassed to write that I lost my temper. What I had communicated was that I valued the car more than him, that I cared more about material things. It wasn't he who had done damage. It was me: I put a substantial ding in our relationship. Or rather, that is what I had risked doing. I apologized to him. "Accidents happen," I said, wiping away his tears. I asked him to forgive me and he nodded and we hugged a long while.

The fact that I still recall that incident vividly so many years later tells me that it was a learning moment—for both of us. Children learn from what we say and do and how we react, and so often, we parent out of emotion. Ask anyone to recall a time long past when he or she spilled juice on a couch, or broke a window with a ball, or some such childhood transgression. You'll hear the stories. Generally, they will involve a lot of yelling, maybe a spanking, and the ones who seem out of control are the adults. The kids are being kids, but the grown-ups aren't being very grown up. They seem interested in possessions more than principles. Our children are watching us closely. In the little things, we teach them well.

# The Lessons of History

Vanderbilt. Carnegie. Gates. Buffett. Bezos. Zuckerberg. Musk. Household names, all of them, along with many others past and present who have reached the monetary mountaintop. Stories of astounding wealth can teach us much about how families can do things right—or not. Once, the emerging technologies of the Industrial Revolution led to great riches. Today, the wealth often derives from the emerging technologies of the Information Age. Now, as then, entrepreneurs have built fortunes—and faced the ethical dilemma of what to do with it all.

In the Gilded Age of the late nineteenth and early twentieth centuries, society saw the advent of the telegraph and telephone, railroads and automobiles, electric light and the dawn of flight. This was an age that produced families of opulent, if not enduring, wealth and generated a philanthropic spirit that cultivated some of the great institutions of the day.

"The man who dies rich dies disgraced," the Pittsburgh steel magnate Andrew Carnegie wrote in a widely read essay, *The Gospel of Wealth*, published in 1889, asserting that the wealthy have a moral obligation to better the community. He wrote that individuals should spend the first part of their lives making as much money as possible and the remainder of their years giving it away. Carnegie was true to his word. His philanthropic example led to an outpouring of funding for parks, libraries, museums, and other institutions and community treasures.

Born the son of a struggling Scottish weaver who sought a better life in America, Carnegie believed that the poor learn a much stronger work ethic and sense of leadership than children of privilege. Those who inherit wealth are more likely to squander it, he warned, suggesting that the money would be far better used to benefit society.

At age sixty-five, he sold Carnegie Steel Company to J.P. Morgan for 480 million dollars. By the end of his life, Carnegie had given most of his fortune away.

To his wife and daughter, he left a relatively modest but comfortable inheritance to which they had agreed years earlier. His wife kept her personal assets, their Manhattan townhouse, their holiday home in Scotland, and a small cash gift. His daughter received a small trust fund. Four generations later, Andrew Carnegie's descendants mostly are self-made professionals—living conservatively, proud of their legacy, and dedicated to the philosophy that life is what we make of it.[1]

Cornelius "Commodore" Vanderbilt, like Carnegie, began with next to nothing. Carnegie's first job, at age thirteen, was in a Pittsburgh cotton factory. Vanderbilt started as a Staten Island boat pilot, expanding to steamboats and then railroads to build a transportation empire. And, also like Carnegie, his descendants today have little of that fortune, but not because the money was given away. It was frittered away.

The Vanderbilt wealth vanished primarily due to luxurious living and rivalry among the heirs. Succeeding generations did generously endow the arts and science and charitable causes, but they also reveled in high-society life, outdoing one another with extravagant mansions along Fifth Avenue in Manhattan and summer "cottages" in Newport, Bar Harbor, and the Berkshires. Much of the wealth went to the upkeep of those edifices, along with yachts, antiques, Old Master artwork, luxury travel, and extravagant dinners and parties.

As the railroad industry came on hard times with freight competition from trucks, barges, and airplanes, an increasing number of heirs continued to keep up appearances without developing the enterprise. A

---

1    Chloe Sorvino, "The gilded age family that gave it all away: the Carnegies," *Forbes*, July 8, 2014, https://www.forbes.com/sites/chloesorvino/2014/07/08/whats-become-of-them-the-carnegie-family.

fortune is destined to fade when spending outstrips income. Cornelius Vanderbilt had built the business to a hundred million dollars. His son, William, doubled the value, then divided the estate among his own sons—and in that third generation, the growth ceased. One of Cornelius' grandsons, William K. Vanderbilt, married a socialite and indulged her rather than focusing on the business. He later remarked that the family money "left me with nothing to hope for, with nothing definite to seek or strive for," according to a biography written by a cousin. "Inherited wealth is a real handicap to happiness."

Today, we hear echoes of those lessons in the stories of modern families that have attained unprecedented wealth. The philanthropic spirit still flourishes, as evidenced by the more than two hundred wealthy individuals and couples who have signed the Giving Pledge, a campaign that Bill Gates of Microsoft and Warren Buffett of Berkshire Hathaway launched in 2010. As of this book's publication, the signatories, from twenty-nine countries, had pledged over half a trillion dollars.

Though the pledge is not legally binding, it is presented as a moral commitment for the rich to "publicly dedicate the majority of their wealth to philanthropy." Among the wealthiest signers, besides Gates and Buffett, are Larry Ellison of Oracle Corporation; Mark Zuckerberg of Facebook; Michael Bloomberg of Bloomberg L.P.; Elon Musk of Tesla and SpaceX; and MacKenzie Scott, the ex-wife of Amazon founder Jeff Bezos. The ultrawealthy Bezos had not signed the pledge as of this book's publication in 2024.

As for the Gates fortune, it is going into the Gates Foundation, the world's largest private charitable organization, thereby escaping the estate tax that would claim about half of the estate if it were left to their children. The children could operate the foundation, but they will not get the money donated to it. Neither will the government. Most of the Gates fortune will benefit tax-exempt charitable interests. And Buffett, too, has earmarked major contributions to the Gates Foundation rather than leaving the money to his family. "There's no reason why future generations of little Buffetts should command society just because they came from the right womb," he has said. "Where's the justice in that?"[2]

Joan Kroc, no doubt, would have agreed. The title of a 2016 biography by Lisa Napoli, *Ray and Joan: The Man Who Made the McDonald's Fortune and the Woman Who Gave It All Away*, sums up her story. Her giving campaign began in earnest after her husband's death in 1984 and culminated in a final rush of philanthropy after learning in 2003 that she had brain cancer and only months to live. The list of about 190 recipients takes up ten pages. The $2.7 billion in bequests from her estate included $1.6 billion to the Salvation Army for community centers in poor neighborhoods—it was the largest one-time donation ever given to a charity—and $235 million to National Public Radio.

Joan Kroc had enjoyed the luxuries of wealth but discovered that it "came not with strings attached, but with ropes," Napoli wrote. "It attracted sycophants, opportunists, and people who believed having an abundance of cash made life better, solved every problem. … She wished she could disabuse people of the idea that money equaled happiness."

Kroc was wise in her decision to leave most of the fortune to a variety of charitable, social, and cultural causes. She earmarked relatively little for individuals, choosing instead to enrich the community in ways that demonstrated deeper values that she deemed worthy of preserving. She did not want to contribute to a generation of lives without purpose.

---

2    "Faces of the week June 26–30, 2006," *Forbes*, June 30, 2006, https://www.forbes.com/2006/06/30/buffett-ellison-ballmer-cx_mm_gl_0630usfaceweek.html#5dfedc397229.

# "Where There Is No Vision..."

A theme throughout this book is that making money makes sense only when it supports clear values. Devoid of a vision, money accomplishes little or nothing. Proverbs 29:18 says, "Where there is no vision, the people will perish." Most businesses have vision and mission statements. Why don't we for our families?

If you ask people what they want for their families, most will say the same sort of things. Beyond just surviving by putting food on the table, having shelter, clothes, and an opportunity to achieve success, they want everyone to get along and to respect one another. They want to become the best version of themselves. They want to do a good job of supporting their loved ones and not just financially. They want to develop strong relationships. Those are fine goals, indeed.

So, the first question to ask yourself is this: How do you move from *wanting* to *doing*? How do you shape the model family that you envision? And the second question: What might be getting in the way of having such a family? Could it be you?

Just after the turn of the millennium, our pastor, Rick Warren, wrote his bestseller *The Purpose Driven Life*, which has sold more than fifty million copies in eighty-five different languages. The book's subtitle is *What on Earth Am I Here For?*—and at one point or another, most of us grapple with that question. Defining a purpose in life and dedicating oneself to pursuing it is not necessarily easy. A walk of faith is not necessarily a smooth one. Trouble comes to all lives, as pastor Warren well knows. Since the death of his son, his church has made strides toward promoting awareness of mental health issues. Out of the pain, we managed to distill a purpose. That's why we are here: to live a life of meaning and service to our fellow humans, each in his or her own way. The book's first sentence is: "It's not about you."

It is that measure of devotion that we must communicate to the next generation. The central values that we bequeath to our heirs will be crucial when they hold the purse strings as the wealthiest generation in history. As I write this, the rate of retirement for baby boomers is ten thousand per day.[3] By 2045, GenXers will have become the primary beneficiaries of the estimated wealth—between $84 and $129 trillion—that U.S. households will transfer to heirs and charity.[4] They will have portfolios swelling with potential to change the world for the better. Potential alone, however, yields nothing. What stirs people to action is commitment. Those who understand the *why* are eager to figure out the *how*. I love Ghandi's words: "Be the change you want to see in the world."

Most of our clients at Apriem Advisors are successful from a worldly perspective. They have accumulated money. Then, along comes the question that strikes to the heart: *Is that all there is?* Our humanity cries out to know that we are here for a reason. Each of us longs for significance and purpose. Each of us wants to matter—and much of the answer to our searching will lie in how well we relate to our families, friends, community. In the richness of our relationships lies our greatest wealth.

As you read further, you will learn more about our unconventional approach to multigenerational wealth management. It is an approach that helps families manage their wealth purposefully to benefit the generations to come. It is an approach that emphasizes the importance of frank dialogue that leads to understanding and unity. That unity doesn't necessarily come on day one. Often, it comes

---

3    David Haass, "Retirement trends of baby boomers," *Forbes*, September 3, 2019, https://www.forbes.com/sites/forbesfinancecouncil/2019/09/03/retirement-trends-of-baby-boomers/#54633c1f7378.

4    Hillary Hoffower and Chloe Berger, "The 'great wealth transfer' isn't $72 trillion but $129 trillion, BofA says—and the government gave most of it to baby boomers," Fortune, October 28, 2023, https://fortune.com/2023/10/28/great-wealth-transfer-baby-boomers-bank-of-america-millennials-government-policy/.

through conversations unfolding over years among family members and between them and their advisor. It develops as families increasingly recognize the responsibility to honor the parents and grandparents who left a legacy of values more precious than gold.

Will the next generation be ready for an infusion of wealth of unprecedented scale? Will the recipients treat that inheritance respectfully and manage it effectively once it is separated from those who earned and stewarded it? Will the transfer of wisdom keep pace with the transfer of wealth? Those are the questions that I often find to be top of mind as I speak with our clients. They lack confidence that their heirs will bring to the table the values that produced and grew the money. I tell my clients that though they can't do much to change widespread societal maladies, they certainly can influence the destiny of their own families. They can make their money matter.

If you'd like to discover your own family's values, I've included a "Discovering My Values" worksheet in Appendix A at the back of the book. Follow along to identify the core values that drive your family's vision and mission. I've also included my own family's values below.

## KONG FAMILY VALUES

FAMILY

FAITH

SERVICE

GENEROSITY

COMMUNITY

# CHAPTER 2

# How Much Is Enough?

---

Warren Buffett understands that a wise steward of family assets will leave to the children "enough money so that they would feel they could do anything, but not so much that they could do nothing."[5] An inheritance certainly can be a springboard to great accomplishments. Sometimes, though, it becomes a trap that squelches ambition and initiative.

In my profession as a wealth manager for several wealthy families, I have met a parade of parents deeply concerned about their children as they come of age. Once the children assume control of the family wealth, will they manage it with the wisdom that it took to make it? Or will they grab the money and run, spending it on sports cars and creature comforts, oblivious to the damage done by market forces and unnecessary taxes? Will the children use the money to launch new

---

5    Richard I. Kirkland Jr., "Should you leave it all to the children?" Fortune, September 29, 1986.

enterprises and build something better for themselves and society—or will they squabble over who got what or who got more and barely speak to one another?

In short, will the wealth breed unity or animosity? Will it build or destroy? Or will it simply stifle? That depends on the family, of course, and how the parents and children view money and relate to one another. Some have a healthy understanding of its proper role in life. For many others, though, no matter how much they amass, it's never enough—because "enough" is always just a little bit more.

To illustrate what can go wrong and what can go right, let me tell you about a few families that I met early in my career.

Tom and Tammy doted on their only daughter and did a masterful job at putting away money in a custodial account for a minor. They wished to ensure that when she reached college age, she would be wanting for nothing. As the couple contributed to that account throughout Gina's childhood, the money grew and grew to $300,000 when she was eighteen years old. Meanwhile, Tom and Tammy had developed other sizable assets to pay Gina's education costs and living needs, so they decided to let her manage the custodial account as she wished. She would be all set to buy a house or start a business when she got older, they figured. It would be their daughter's seed money for success in life, and they felt proud to hand over the reins. Though they could have waited until she was twenty-five, they officially granted her ownership of the account on her eighteenth birthday.

"Sweetie, look who's all grown up now!" Tammy told her as they dined at an upscale restaurant to celebrate her birthday. She then presented Gina with the account documents wrapped in a bow. Tom leaned over and whispered in her ear, "You go out there and make it happen!" Mom and Dad smiled at her proudly. Gina smiled back.

The three of them still were glowing when they came into my office. "Yup, this is what we want to do," Tom assured me as he signed off on the account and put it in Gina's name. "We've taught her the meaning of money. We can trust our girl." He then offered a few fatherly words about cash management and the importance of investing. They set up the account with a debit card. She picked it up, speechless. "We'll show you how that thing works, too," Tammy said with a wink.

Tom and Tammy were wrong about a few things. For one, their daughter was not all grown up now. For another, she wasn't all that interested in college. And though Gina did go out to make something happen, it wasn't quite what they imagined.

About a month later, a distraught Tammy called me. "Harmon, our daughter has gone off the deep end. How can we shut down that account?"

Tammy explained that Tom had found a list of transactions on Gina's statement. The numbers told a startling story. She had become a regular on Melrose Avenue, shopping and partying with the Hollywood and Beverly Hills crowd. She had been paying the tab at fancy restaurants for groups of admiring friends. The account was bleeding thousands upon thousands of dollars.

"I confronted Gina about this," Tammy told me, "but she just says, 'This money is *mine*, Mom.' She keeps saying she deserves her privacy. What are we going to do?"

"I know how you must feel," I said, "and that's just awful. Legally, though, there's nothing you can do. She's right. It's her money now—always has been, really, but you gave her all the rights of access to it at age eighteen."

Sadder but wiser were Tammy and Tom—and no doubt Gina, too, once she discovered how easy it is to burn through more than a quarter of a million dollars. In their eyes, she was a good kid who would never disappoint Mom and Dad. In her eyes, she had just won the lotto. Her parents had tried to make her responsible by sheer willpower. They had let her know that they were taking good care of her and had plenty of other resources to get her through college, so she could use this money to make her own financial decisions. And she did—until it was gone.

Let's switch now to another scene, another family that I was privileged to know along the way. This couple, too, had done well and grown sizable portfolios. Bob and Ann had two smart and ambitious sons, Danny and Kevin. Danny went to the University of Southern California (USC) to become a dentist, and Kevin went to the University of California, Los Angeles (UCLA) to become a pharmacist. Good schools, both—but neither son felt certain their parents could afford the tuition. They asked, but they didn't get an answer. "Just think about your studies for now," each was told. "We'll sit down with you later on and figure out the rest."

Bob and Ann visited me as they were preparing to send the older son, Danny, off to his freshman year. "Yeah, we haven't clued them in to how much money we have," Bob told me. "And neither knows we've also set aside hundreds of thousands in their own names. Last thing we want is a couple brats who think money is no object."

Ann nodded and smiled. "Ever hear people say USC means *University of Spoiled Children*? No way will ours be one of them!"

After finishing his first year, Danny approached his parents. "I need a car. I feel out of place. All the other kids have these new BMWs and whatnot, and here I am taking the bus."

"Look, your dad and I can't afford to get you something like that," Ann told him. They could, but Danny didn't need to know that. "But yeah, get a car. Look for a used one, and we'll figure out together how to pay for it." Danny shopped around, got a good deal on some sweet wheels a few years old, and Mom and Dad agreed to cover the modest cost. The price wasn't the point. They just wanted to see that their sons understood the value of a dollar.

I had to chuckle when Bob and Ann told me that story. "You know they're going to figure out pretty soon, after they graduate and get a job, how much money they've had all along. I can imagine the look on their faces when they get their 1099s at tax time and ask what's up with all those dividends and interest they get to pay taxes on. What are you going to tell them? *Oh, that's just the earnings on $500,000 or so we set aside for each of you kids?* They'll either adore you or lash out at you, perhaps experiencing both emotions simultaneously."

Both sons have since become Apriem clients, and they each have grown accounts of over a few million dollars while still in their thirties. They don't dip into that money. Both live modestly off the income of good jobs. They learned well, and not just in college. Danny and Kevin grew up in a family that did not focus on money even though they had plenty of it—and that grounding carried through into adulthood. They also pursued academic careers that they love and are passionate about. Many parents suggest or even insist their kids to study something that will earn them a great living. That sounds like practical, sound advice, yet the young people can end up hating their careers as life seems like a ride on a very nice merry-go-round that's not really going anywhere.

## The Questions Get Harder

The daughter in the first story didn't think she was doing anything wrong. Gina figured she was rich and could afford to spend $200 on a pair of jeans or $100 for sunglasses and treat her friends to a night on the town. Losing all that money in her custodial account might have been a blessing in disguise if she learned a hard lesson to keep her from squandering the millions that she would inherit. Gina, perhaps, just needed a better education on family finance, which is hard to come by in our school systems, even at the college level. Maybe she just needed time to mature.

What nobody needs, at age eighteen, is the impression that money is inexhaustible. Even in a family with strong values and good communication, that's a tender age to face such a worldly temptation. Many people go through life without ever reaching a level of financial sophistication and self-control to do well with wealth—so how can that be expected of a teenager?

A lot of parents open an account in the child's name, presuming that's the best way to set aside college money that he or she will need someday. They don't stop to think that a regular investment account can be used for any purpose once that child becomes an adult. There are a variety of other ways to save efficiently for college and stipulate that the money can be used only for that purpose. Parents need to address the financial risk of a kid becoming an adult without acting like one. Giving a teenager power over a pile of money is a good idea only if it's a test run for the big inheritance down the road.

Can too much money spoil the child? Yes. It's a clear risk that can erase wealth when that child becomes an adult, at least nominally, and assumes control of the assets. The risk is as real as the market taking a dive, and it has happened time and time again. Parents can mitigate that risk, but first, they must be aware of it, and then they must equip the next generation to manage such a serious responsibility. Without financial knowledge and the right values, the kids are likely to blow it. They will succumb to the "me first" culture, unwilling to defer gratification.

The young people in those two scenarios were not the only ones who learned something from those experiences. I did too. My wife and I agreed that we would not be sharing with our children how much we were saving through the years for their education. They would learn the balance only when it was time to turn the money over to them—and we would do whatever we could to make sure they were ready to handle that information.

When I was a teenager, not only did I have to work to buy my own car, but when it broke down, I bought the shop manual to figure out how to repair it myself. It was a given that my parents would not grant me a new car upon request. There was no question. Today, I work with families where the big question is: *Should I buy my kid a new fancy car because I can?* Greater wealth does not make the money questions easier. It often makes them harder.

## Helpful or Hurtful?

In our society, many families of wealth struggle over how much money to put in the hands of the next generation and when. Young people sometimes act as if a generous inheritance is their birthright, and their parents feel pangs of guilt at the thought of withholding it. In truth, by giving them too much of a "head start," they could end up forever denying their sons and daughters the satisfaction and sense of accomplishment of earning a paycheck.

A simple principle is at work here: Just because you can do something doesn't mean you should. I knew a wealthy widow who struggled with that principle. Eleanor had to face the question of how much, if anything, was enough for her daughter, whom it seemed no amount of money could help.

The daughter, Nora, was lost in a fog of drugs. At times, she had been living on the streets. Eleanor was at wits' end, spending whatever it took to get Nora in and out of rehab and living decently, but nothing seemed to work.

Eleanor also had a son, Barry, a responsible young man with a good job. Mom felt conflicted about how to divide the estate. She had $5–$7 million to distribute upon her passing, but she realized that if she split it equally, half would likely vanish and most likely feed Nora's drug addiction. She suggested to Barry that his sister's half be put in a trust for her benefit—and would he be so kind as to agree to be the gatekeeper?

If that sounds like a reasonable solution, imagine how it would play out. Barry wanted no part of the arrangement. He did not wish to be put in the position of deciding how much Nora would get and when. He, too, had been trying to help his sister, and he feared that playing that role would put strain on their relationship and ultimately destroy their sibling bond.

And so, both of them kept paying her way, propping her up financially, getting her through rehab. Last I heard, mother and son were still hoping beyond hope that this time would be different. Both were struggling with that big question of how much is enough and how to maintain a relationship that is troubled. Barry found himself wondering whether any amount would be too much for an addict. He suggested to his mother that Nora's half of the estate might best go to charity someday. Nothing had been decided, but their story shows how complicated money decisions can be.

Such a dilemma is inconceivable to many parents. "That won't happen in my family," they say, until it does. Most of us know someone caught in the grip of addiction or mental health issues. It seems no family is immune. Still, I often am surprised when people bring in their trust documents that simply provide for the children to receive, say, a third at age eighteen, a third at age twenty-five, and the remainder at thirty, without any further stipulations. "What if your child becomes a drug addict," I ask, "or develops a psychosis, or is a victim in an abusive relationship?"

Parents need to consider what they don't want to hear. No matter how confident they feel about their Billy, what if they died in an accident and orphaned him at age twelve? Grieving and angry and entering adolescence without parents to guide him, that young man easily could go astray yet still stake his claim in a few years on the life insurance payoff. Dear old Uncle Joe, as trustee of the account, would be telling him, "I know you're messed up on meth, so here's a few hundred thousand dollars to start with." Without a means of controlling the flow, nobody would ever be able to tell Billy that "enough is enough," either of drugs or money.

When couples tell themselves that they want the kids to be all right, they really mean that they want them to turn out all right. They often confuse financial support with moral guidance, feeling obligated to the former when in truth it's the latter that the next generation so badly needs. Even young people who are well-grounded sometimes make big mistakes before coming to their senses. Throwing money at them certainly won't make them turn out all right. It's likely to do quite the opposite.

The kids will turn out all right when they respect the power of money and appreciate the years of work and sacrifice that go into generating it. They will turn out all right if Mom and Dad behave like parents and not pals. They'll turn out all right when someone cares enough to ensure that they are prepared.

When the children are not ready to steward the family assets, the consequences are sad. Countless times, the old expression "shirtsleeves to shirtsleeves in three generations" has proved to be true. The concept is so ingrained in human nature that many cultures around the world have some version of that saying. The first generation rises from the factories or fields to build wealth in a white-collar world. The second generation lives well but learns little, and the money slips away until the children of the third generation find themselves back in the fields or factories, sleeves rolled up, sweating out a living. So easily, a family can forget what it's like to be broke—and that's what destines it to be broke again. Seventy percent of wealthy families lose their fortune by the second generation, according to a study conducted by the Williams Group, an advisory firm that assists families with wealth transfer. Ninety percent lose it by the third generation. The study tracked more than 3,200 high-net-worth families.[6] I actually spoke with the author, Amy Castoro, of this study. She told me that many of these families had a full team of advisors and lawyers. Despite all of this, the next generations failed. So, if wealthy families fail in this, what hope is there for the average family of more modest means?

The lesson should be clear: Family leaders bear a responsibility to show their children the way—to talk to them, mentor them, encourage them, but never pamper them. Finding the right balance is not necessarily easy, but the message comes through when conversation flows readily. When young people buy in to the passion of the parents and grandparents, and when they experience for themselves the dedication and hard work required to build wealth, they will be well-situated to excel.

When parents try to pay to make troubles go away, they find them multiplying. Frustrated over family issues, they turn their attention to what they know they can do well, which is making more money.

---

6    Catey Hill, "Here's why 90% of rich people squander their fortunes," MarketWatch.com, April 23, 2017, https://www.marketwatch.com/amp/story/guid/D49C9049-792E-42EF-B46F-ADEC4CA3B2D0.

They buckle down on a career or a business, spending even less time developing those family relationships which, in the end, will be what matter most.

# Better to Inherit or Earn?

Until you know how much is enough for yourself, you cannot know what is right for your heirs. If you are nearing retirement age and aren't sure you have enough to get you through, then you need to find out. If you are investing too aggressively for someone your age, you likely should be taking a more protective stance. However, if you are confident that you have more than you will ever need yourself, then it's time to decide what happens to the remainder when you are gone.

Having plenty of money to go around does not make the inheritance question easier. Wealthy parents may see their grown children as irresponsible or aimless, spending foolishly, and worry that their grandchildren are on a path to trouble—so why fortify a bad situation? People treat money that they inherit very differently than money that they earn. Why encourage low standards or questionable morality? Caring parents have higher expectations for their life savings. For those who have attained a degree of wealth, it's not a matter of "where will the money come from?" It's "where will the money go?"

Think of it this way: If you have been blessed with abundance in life, why not bequeath a healthy portion of your resources to your descendants two hundred years hence? Would that be wise? Yes, if "abundance" means love and a strong sense of values. You would want that to linger for generations. But if abundance just means money, why would you risk ruining the lives of relatives so distant down the line who probably will never even know your name or how you built those resources. You might as well give a fortune to strangers without a thought as to what they will do with it.

A wealthy businessman, Brandon, came to see me recently when the federal exemption level on estate taxes—about $5 million at the time for an individual, or about $10 million for a married couple—was scheduled to expire and revert to a much lower level. The government ended up extending the exemption, but many wealthy families were scrambling in the meantime to get money out of their estate to avoid the painful 40 percent levy. Tax attorneys were doing brisk business drafting documents and collecting hefty fees from their panicky clients. Brandon was one of them. He was preparing to set aside $10 million in a complex estate plan that included a special dynasty trust which would grow and grow for future generations he had yet to meet.

"So is this a good idea, or what?" he asked me.

"It's an idea," I said. "And, sure, it's one way to keep Uncle Sam out of your family fortune. But just one question: Are you and your wife aware of the long-term implications this decision will have on your future family?"

He hesitated, then smiled. "I guess I was hoping you'd explain that to me." An astute businessman, he also was wise enough to know what he didn't know.

"Well, this decision isn't so much for you as it is for future generations within your bloodline. One day, your kids could get something. Your grandchildren, too, and your great grandkids. And hey, someday those trust funds might grow to $100 million for a future generation you'll never meet or know anything about."

"I hadn't thought of it that way," he said.

"Trusts certainly have their place," I said, "and financially, what your tax lawyer is suggesting does make sense. But first just ask yourself if this is what you want as your legacy, a massive amount of money to be consumed by people whose beliefs and lifestyle might not be remotely like yours. Is that what you really want to do?" It wasn't. Brandon gave up the whole idea. It didn't align with his values. He could have afforded to take that step, but he recognized that just because he could didn't mean he should. He did not want his legacy to be about funding a silver spoon generation.

## Changing the Conversation

One day years ago, a real estate millionaire named Cameron visited my office. He told me that he had a $30 million portfolio and wondered whether I might be interested in managing it. Just one thing though: First, I had to prove myself worthy.

Cameron had approached several other firms and dangled his millions in front of their money managers to see how much they salivated. "I'm going to choose five of them that seem the hungriest," he told me, "and each will get $6 million of my money to see who can grow it the most by the end of the year." He added, "And the one that does the best will get all my business."

I didn't say a word. He studied me. "You game?" he asked.

"I really don't think we're a good fit," I told him. He was shocked. I politely escorted him to the door. I could have accepted his suggestion. After all, there was nothing to lose and much to gain—namely, a large account to manage. But I was dismayed at his attitude toward money. Why would he put all his net worth into a race? He would no doubt be subjecting it to dangerous market risk as investment firms aggressively vied for the prize.

This was a man who was in it for sport. Cameron was a gambler, not an investor, and to me, it was clear that he never had wrestled with the question of "how much is enough?" He fit the pattern of people who get bored with life and look for ways to find significance. And I also knew that even if we "won" the race, there would just be another race, then another, and another. He was shooting for as much as possible.

Cameron was in his early seventies at the time. That's an age when smart investors tend to think more conservatively, taking a protective stance with the proceeds of their life's work. He had much more than he needed personally, and he could have put the rest to good use in a world of countless needs rather than exposing it to high-risk, winner-take-all race. The economic "law of diminishing marginal utility" asserts that wealthy people reach a point where further gain does not bring greater satisfaction and happiness. When they have more than they will ever need, their money loses its utility. Making more of it will not enhance their own lives. Cameron had crossed that line long ago, and he didn't know it.

I have encountered other investors who subject a fortune to high-risk securities for no good reason. They have plenty of money, but they crave more, as if their net worth determines their self-worth. They treat the markets like a casino. Greedy people can become wealthy, but the lust for money also can land them in the poorhouse. The latter is more likely. And if a high-stakes and high-stress approach works for one generation, what about the next? The dice might not roll the same way for the children. If they continue that pattern, the odds are that they will lose it all.

As my colleagues and I work with people on their family wealth management plans, we help them to discover the essential sense of purpose behind their financial decisions so they can invest at a risk level appropriate to their situation and aspirations. That awakening doesn't come overnight, and many issues and details must be addressed along the way. Any family that is building assets needs guidance in three broad areas: how to effectively accumulate wealth in keeping with their life goals; how to preserve that wealth so that a market crash, inflation, and other risks don't steal it; and how to develop a cash flow for retirement so they can continue their accustomed lifestyle and fulfill their dreams.

Though it would be wise to start early—those three areas represent the beginning, middle, and finale of one's financial life—people often come to see us for a specific reason. They are experiencing some big change. They are about to get a lot of money from the sale of a business, for example. Perhaps a spouse has died, or they are facing some other crisis. Maybe they wake up one day and see how close they are to retirement and aren't sure they can swing it. A husband and wife realize that one or the other is likely to live at least twenty or thirty more years, and they haven't calculated whether their money will last. What if one or both get sick? Their heads spin with all the what-if's. Though seeking guidance sooner would have been better, they are smart enough to know what they don't know.

Often, those who come seeking help don't know quite where to start the conversation, but they have observed the destructive influence of too much affluence in the families of some of their friends and want to fend off any harm to their own children. Sometimes, they ask me to do what amounts to an early intervention. They see their kids heading into life without good money habits, so they come to us with a plea: "Can you talk to our kids? Can you help to get them situated?" Sure, we can talk to them, and set up a financial plan, too, but getting situated doesn't just mean financially comfortable. It means possessing the wherewithal to manage one's own affairs wisely, self-directed and self-assured.

Though most parents are not struggling with problem children, they still feel conflicted about the inheritance. In working with them, I try to cut through the confusion. I often hear this: "We want to leave enough to our kids so that they will never need anything"—but they cannot articulate how much that might be. A million dollars? Five million? They don't know.

Couples who have more than one child may wonder how to divide the wealth among the siblings so as not to trigger resentments. If one child has been deeply involved in the family business while another has chosen an entirely different career, who will take over the enterprise? Not all the children may share the passion that built the wealth, but they understandably will care about the wealth itself. An equal division doesn't always make sense. What's fair?

Is equal the same as fair in a dynamic family situation? We held a family meeting with my now adult children. I asked them if they believe we treated them equally. They answered with a confident, "Yes, of course, Dad."

"What if I told you we did not treat you equally?"

"What do you mean, Dad?"

I explained how it cost us thousands of dollars for Haley to do competitive cheer from middle school to high school, yet we paid significantly less for Troy and Kyle who chose to do track and field. So, I asked them if I should somehow make up the difference in cash to make things more equal. Of course, they agreed that was not necessary and sounded ludicrous. So then, I summarized that we treated them fair but not equal in terms of the family finances. My point was, when they become the stewards of our finances, I wanted them to remember this conversation. I have witnessed many siblings fight over their parents' past decision about how money was spent on each of them. Family unity is far more important than who gets what and when.

The key is to ask these questions and have the conversations in the first place. Frustrated, many families can find it easier not to talk about those issues or think about them. They keep putting off what they fear will be a difficult discussion, but that only keeps the tensions simmering. All so unnecessary. A simple conversation is all it takes to clarify expectations and preserve family unity. Unfortunately, when they do see an advisor, the conversation often continues in the vein of "more is better," the mantra of our consumer society. Many financial advisors hold that world view, and so the conversation begins and ends with how to better the bottom line.

A far better approach to the money conversation addresses the bigger picture, but generally it will start with a focus on some details. My colleagues and I first address the issue at hand, the main reason for the meeting, because that's what is heavy on their minds. We must resolve it before turning to the deeper conversations. It's like Maslow's hierarchy: The basic human needs come before the higher pursuits. Often the worry is unfounded, and people are faring better than they imagined, but doubts can run deep even in highly affluent families. Once they feel reassured of financial security, we can look further at the details—the investments, the taxes, the risk management, the estate issues, the cash flow, and more. It is true that nobody can avoid death and taxes, but one still must take the right steps to deal with both.

The conversation typically then turns to the children. Sometimes, we hear something like this: "We're afraid they will make terrible decisions and the money will hurt them more than help them, but we really don't know what to do about that." Or: "We trust that they will do well with our money, but how can we do that without paying a ton of taxes." Two different perspectives, both focusing on what is best for the children. One perspective worries they will get too much, but the other worries they won't get enough. The first attitude tells me that at least they have taken a hard look at what might happen. It's the latter perspective that concerns me more.

Eventually, we get to the premise of the conversation, the bigger, long-term picture—the *why* that governs the *what* and the *how*. None of those details can make sense without grasping the reason for accumulating all that money. Before they get anything to live *on*, children need something to live *for*. As we discussed in chapter 1, strong values should be the foundation for every financial decision. Families without a clear vision are families adrift. Without guiding principles, they lack the simplicity to make sense of the complexities.

The fundamental question comes down to this: Where will the money do the most good, and how can you keep it from doing harm? In seeking the answer, we talk with families about how they view money and its role in their lives and in the world. We get people to think about what they really will be leaving behind for generations to come. We change the conversation to the things that matter most.

## While There's Still Time

Martha was a retired widow who was worth millions. As she got older, she mused from time to time about possibly taking her children's families on a cruise together. It would be a delightful time with loved ones and pure joy for the grandkids.

"But I just don't know, that's a lot of money," she told me when she came to visit one day. "Things just cost so much these days." This was a truly frugal woman who, despite her wealth, had been content to live on her Social Security checks.

I pointed out to her that she had enough resources to pay for that trip and many others.

"Yeah, but I don't want to touch any of that money because who knows what might come up. I might need it, and then what? And besides, I want everything to go to the kids and grandkids. It's going to be theirs, and I shouldn't just be spending it."

"Maybe you can think of it as an investment," I told her. "It's an investment in your relationships with your family. You're healthy and strong now. Wait too long, and they might be taking that cruise someday without you."

"Well, yeah, I know all that, but…" Her voice trailed off. "Maybe next year I'll take another look," she said, before changing the subject.

The next year came and went, and another, and the cruise didn't happen. One day, Martha suffered a serious fall and required extended therapy. It would be a long time, if ever, before she could even consider going on a trip with her family. A few years later, she died with a very large estate and leaving millions in inheritance having never taken that family trip with her kids and grandkids.

To be financially responsible is wise, of course, and good stewards do their best to multiply their money. They save and invest it, but they do not simply stockpile it for who knows what. They understand that money matters only because of what it represents. Since the dawn of civilization, it has been a means for exchanging things of value—and a cherished time with one's family certainly is a thing of value. A fond memory is a thing of value.

Without a clear purpose, building a portfolio is just a numbers game. Some people play the game too aggressively, taking big risks to make big gains that they do not need. Others play too cautiously, so fearful of losses that they miss out on opportunities. Sometimes, people hold back out of concern that they might not have enough to last. They just don't know. Other times, though, possibly because they once knew a time of want, people will hoard a fortune and postpone the making of memories—until it is too late.

Today, while there's still time, let's talk. How much is enough for yourself and for your heirs? My simple answer—and I'm sure that Mr. Buffett would agree—is "enough to help but not to hurt." That principle, however, encompasses many variables and nuances that family members need to discover and explore as they sit together at the table and get the conversation rolling.

# CHAPTER 3

# The Price of Everything and the Value of Nothing

"Dad made us live like paupers!" exclaimed the young heiress, Jennifer, who came to see me to talk about some financial and life decisions. "Mom and I had no idea how much money he had. He kept a lid on all that—and he wouldn't even let her remodel the kitchen!"

A few years earlier, upon inheriting several million dollars after her father died, Jennifer had decided that she, for one, would not hoard money. She would put it to good use—and for her that translated, at first at least, into good times. She was a single mom with two kids, Emma and John, and she was determined to give them a wealth of good memories.

Nobody could have accused Jennifer of being a miser, but she was leaning toward the other extreme. And she realized it. She had been trying to make up for lost time. She wanted to reclaim some of the things that she felt her father unfairly had denied the family—but she found that she could not buy joy. She came to talk with me when she started feeling bored by it all. She wanted something more and not for herself. Putting the money to good use did not mean just spending it. It meant giving the money a purpose.

"I'm tired of all these trips and hotels," she said. "It's time for a change. I want to set a good example for Emma and John. I know Dad thought he was setting a good example for me, but I just ended up feeling mad at him for being tight-fisted. I sure don't want my kids to be mad at me someday, thinking I was a spendthrift."

We began talking about how her experiences growing up had influenced her perception of money. In her heart of hearts, Jennifer wanted to know that money had some significant value outside of the bank account. We looked at a variety of charitable causes that she might support and organizations where she might volunteer time and resources, and we talked about tax-efficient ways that she could contribute and make a big difference in people's lives.

Her father had meant well. He felt his mission was to get his family to embrace frugal values. Unfortunately, he did not leave much room for his wife and daughter to express their views. He put a lot of effort into building a fortune but not so much into building relationships. He never found the right balance.

As a result, resentments needlessly took root. Jennifer knew that her dad wasn't a bad man, but he didn't know how to build unity in his family. Good family financial management also requires effective communication. If Jennifer and her parents had regularly sat down together for family meetings to get it all out on the table, a lot of hard feelings could have been avoided.

I had a client, Paul, who similarly wanted to set a good example for his three children. They were grown and had families of their own, and he wanted them to learn to invest responsibly.

At the time (2002–2005), the maximum annual gift allowance was $11,000 for an individual, so Paul wanted to give $22,000 every year to each of the three couples, totaling $66,000 annually. I reassured him that he had sufficient wealth to easily afford to do so. The gifting would also reduce his potential estate tax.

"Invest this money for your future," he told each of his children. Along with the checks, he sent them investment articles that he had cut out. He had been doing this for several years when one day he got a call from one of his sons.

"Dad, we were just wondering, will you be sending us the $22,000 again this year?"

"I expect so, son," Paul answered. He paused. "Why?"

"We just wanted to be careful, you know? We thought we ought to make sure the money was coming, since you've been doing it for a few years now."

"What are you going to do with that money?" Paul asked.

"See, there's this boat I've had my eye on. It's a beauty, Dad, wait till you see it! They want a pretty big down payment, but I figured I'd best hold off until I make sure I have enough."

Paul blew a fuse. I don't know what he said, but I know what he was thinking: *Boy, you're not the only one who's going to be holding off! You want a boat, go buy it with your own money.*

"I just don't get it," Paul told me later. "How could I have been clearer about what I expected? This has got to stop now. I'm having my lawyer rewrite my trust so none of them gets a penny unless they keep working to age sixty-five—after all, that's what I did, and they can, too. I can't have my money helping them to be lazy."

As you might imagine, all three of his children and their families resented being suddenly cut off from that modest flow of money. Dad "gave" it to them with the unwritten stipulation that they invest it, but they did not understand that. He still considered the money to be his own and wanted some control over it and over them.

By rewriting the trust, Paul risked turning exasperation into alienation all around—not only between him and his children, but also among the siblings who considered it unfair that all would be punished for the actions of one. The son who wanted to buy a boat never got a chance to explain that he considered it an investment in memories. He had imagined them all having fun together on family outings. Investment is not just about money. Quality time with your family too is an admirable value. Of course, it's debatable whether a new boat is needed for family quality time to occur.

The anger and resentment on both sides might have been avoided if everyone had come to the table regularly for family meetings aimed at understanding one another and their motivations. Family discord often arises from money issues that better communication could resolve.

# Chatter Matters

The dinner table once was a centerpiece of our culture. Getting together daily for meals was a regular part of family life. Mom and Dad and the kids, and perhaps grandma and grandpa, passed the potatoes and talked about their day. They told stories about yesteryear and shared dreams for tomorrow. As the elders talked about what mattered most to them, the children watched and listened. Family dinners were the one place where families always came together to share a meal and talk.

In today's grab-and-go culture, those times together often get sacrificed to the demands of daily schedules. Mom and Dad rush off to their obligations and come home too weary for words, and the kids, too, get caught up in the shuffle from school to soccer practice to homework to summer camp. Trying to make every minute count, many families allot little time for togetherness. To make matters worse, our so-called "connected" world of social media disconnects them further.

Nonetheless, something about the dinner table—and the entire kitchen, for that matter—calls to people at a primal level. It is as if we still yearned to gather around the fire for the feast, telling the tales handed down to us. The kitchen is a social place. At Apriem Advisors, we have outfitted our office lobby with a kitchen like feel that includes a refrigerator, sink, coffee bar, and a large island counter. We keep the television tuned to the cooking channel. The atmosphere encourages visitors to be open and talkative. Before our remodeling, we had a lobby furnished in dark cherrywood with a television playing market news on CNBC and the tables lined with financial magazines and newspapers. That might seem fitting—but to many visitors already feeling anxious, it was an atmosphere that signaled stress.

My mom always made sure that our family had meals together, no matter what. Nobody ate until all could be gathered around the table, and the television was off. My wife was raised that way, too, and we kept that tradition in our own family. We considered our meal time to be sacred. That was when we each had a chance to talk about the highs and lows of our day, comparing notes, commiserating, and celebrating, sharing the details of daily life. We didn't let the digital world interfere. Pulling out a cell phone at dinnertime was a sure way to lose that privilege. In many families today, the focus is less on conversation and more on digital communication. A family might be assembled at the table, but they are not truly together.

The table where you eat the most meals at in your home is a natural gathering place; it's also a natural place to conduct family meetings. For those who wonder how to get started on conducting those meetings, the dinner table can make the atmosphere feel less formal and less intimidating, especially if the family already is accustomed to sharing meals together. Turning mealtime into meeting time becomes an easy transition.

That only will happen, though, when a family leader declares that *this is what we will do*. Parents need to establish the expectations and consistently adhere to them. Otherwise, they will be sacrificing some of the most precious moments that a family can have together.

Relationships deepen over dinner. As the family members share their stories, observations, and views, they gain a greater understanding of one another. They will not agree on everything, of course, and those differing perspectives are healthy so long as the family strives for a unity. Though not everyone will be of the same mind, they should all be of the same heart. They should treat one another with dignity. This is where we can all learn to agree to disagree at times, and that is okay! However, disagreeing while breaking the unity of the family is not okay; these are the family rules.

The concept that "we are family" should prevail, even when the issues are challenging and might feel divisive. That requires good communication as well as patience, humility, and grace, so that disagreement never slips into a broken relationship. Sometimes, words get said during the heat of emotion and inflict wounds that may fester unless all agree that family comes first. With the balm of forgiveness, those wounds can heal without scars. Striving for family unity can also be great preparation for building unity in our communities and elsewhere.

Our family enjoys watching the television show *The Profit*, in which host Marcus Lemonis attempts to turn around troubled small businesses. He often discovers many of the poorly run companies are a result of dysfunctional family relationships. I particularly recall an episode in which Marcus told one of the business owners, whose passion for the profession had turned to obsession, to forget about the failing restaurant business and pay attention to his troubled family. Lemonis often points out that the heartbeat of a good business is the family, and a business cannot succeed without a successful family life.

Having worked with many family businesses, I must agree with Lemonis that fortunes fade when relationships suffer. Nothing is worth pursuing if it tears loved ones apart. Unbridled ambition can do that. So can the love of money over the love of people. As Oscar Wilde observed, so many people know the price of everything and the value of nothing. They fail to take care of what matters most. Family dysfunctions can destroy the financial potential that could do so much more good. From the start of Apriem, we decided we would commit to not build the business on the backs of our families. Family always came first, then work.

The family leaders have a responsibility to guide the discussions around the table so that important matters are not lost in the details and drama of daily life. That's not to say that the small talk is unimportant. The chatter matters, because you have to start somewhere. And often big talk comes out of small talk. Everyone should get a chance to talk about their day, the good and the bad, in a freewheeling and open atmosphere. Talking about those experiences often yields opportunities to take a deeper dive in a family meeting.

As parents encourage their children to express their views, the goal is not to create clones but rather to reinforce family values and gain a consensus that those values are important. In effect, the family leaders set the agenda of "this is what we stand for" while encouraging independent thinking. They should make sure everyone is on the same page, even if the children are reading at different levels. If you haven't already, now is the time to define your family's values.

When Mom and Dad speak candidly about their feelings and impressions, the kids will feel comfortable doing the same. A good way for Mom and Dad to illustrate the values they wish to instill is to tell stories about how they have dealt with situations in their past. Kids not only will enjoy the tales, and probably ask to hear them again and again, but they also will be getting valuable guidance on how to deal with life's challenges. For kids of any age, storytelling is an effective way to make a point. We adults still enjoy a good story. In Hawaiian culture, we say, "Talk story," which means sitting down with food and drink and sharing stories of fond memories with each other.

Children will feel reassured when they see that their parents stand together on the important issues. Of course, disagreements are common for any couple, but when it comes to the big stuff, the parents need to present a unified front. If they have yet to come to terms on the fundamentals, they should work them out somewhere besides the dinner table. Arguing in front of the kids teaches them that is the way to settle matters. In some families, the kids don't want to come to the table because Mom and Dad are fighting all the time. They would rather stay in their rooms. In such an atmosphere, you couldn't expect to conduct a productive family meeting. Little will be accomplished unless everyone in the family perceives the dinner table as a safe place to speak openly.

# Getting Started

In so many aspects of life, getting started is the hardest part. You might want to get in better shape, for example, but the biggest obstacle is getting to the gym. I often have met people who understand the importance of family meetings but have yet to hold one. It's something new to them, and they don't know where to begin. They are searching for an action step. First things first: It's never too late to begin, even after the kids are grown adults.

If family meetings are new to you and difficult to start, you may consider a trusted third party to facilitate the initial meeting to get things started. This person can provide that jumpstart and set the family on the right path. I frequently have offered to facilitate meetings, typically when it becomes clear to me that a family will benefit greatly by sitting down together for some honest and open dialogue.

When I suggest a family meeting, people often like the idea but want to know how to set it up and the topics that would be appropriate to cover. They also often wonder how much information they should share with their children, young adult kids, or kids' spouses. Much depends on their age, maturity, of course, and the family dynamics. The family needs to determine what to discuss and not discuss and decide on a time frame, expectations, and meeting goals. In our family, we made sure that phones were put away to prevent interruptions. We gave each of us ample time to talk without interruptions or snap judgments, and we always ended with positive words of affirmation for one another. We also developed a one-page document that each of us completed ahead of the meeting to keep us all on track (see "Family Goal Sheet" in Appendix C). Our family meetings were initially about an hour. But today, since we have so much to discuss, and we all have the gift of gab, they can last for hours with meal breaks in between. I view our long meetings as a good thing because it's important that everyone in the family is heard.

The presence of a trusted third party guiding a family meeting makes it objective and often easier to approach difficult topics or the elephants in the room. Finding agreeable solutions is likely to take more than one meeting. The facilitator's role is to get family members talking and to empower them to continue talking. Once they see how an effective meeting is structured and take responsibility for keeping an open dialogue, a neutral meeting facilitator may no longer be necessary.

Once under way, the family meetings need to continue regularly—and not just when some big issue is at hand. Many of us remember how it felt to get called to the principal's office. That generally was not a good thing. Family meetings can feel that way if they take place only in the face of some crisis or looming issue. It's like when the boss strides out of his office and announces, "Everyone into the conference room, and I mean *now*." When everyone has become conditioned to cringing, a meeting is not likely to start out well. That happens in many families: *Dad's calling a meeting, here comes trouble!*

It is human nature to avoid the things we dread. A family meeting, like an office meeting, should not be a venue for reviewing everything that everyone has done wrong. It should be a place primarily for encouragement, not complaints. Family meetings should be conducted regularly so that they become a part of family life. One of the goals of having those meetings is to ensure that the conversation comes easily—and they become easier to do when you do them often.

When families develop the discipline of regular and intentional meetings, they are better able to deal with the tough stuff when it comes along. The family already has established a safe forum for those conversations. Regular meetings become part of the family culture, just as they become part of a business culture. Everyone expects to get regular updates and an opportunity to be heard.

When our children were small, we conducted family meetings about once a month. When they got a little older, we went to quarterly meetings. Sometimes, we held them at the dinner table, and sometimes, boardroom style, more formally. We had some of them during family vacations. Now that our kids are out of the nest and with a few married, our meetings have become more like annual retreats, although we will touch base regularly on important matters as they come up. We all know that we are there for one another.

Among my firm's clients, some ask us to facilitate an annual family meeting for them, which is good, but our expectation is that they also continue to hold regular meetings throughout the year. That is essential to keep the communication flowing, particularly if the family needs to build a better rapport. Otherwise, there is less time for praise and productive planning as the troubles at hand get most of the attention. The family members should look forward to those meetings. They should not feel as if they are walking down the hallway to the principal's office.

# Overcoming Dysfunction

I encourage family meetings, especially when I see an obvious dysfunction that has been getting in the way of a family's progress. Even families that seem to have it all together can feel stymied over some tough issue. Communication might even break down entirely.

I have observed situations, for example, in which the father dominates the conversation while the rest of his family just nods and listens. He comes on strong and thinks he is making progress—but that is because he's the only one talking. He might make a pretense of seeking consensus—*So we're all in agreement on that, right?*—and probably considers himself to be a strong leader, but really, he is ruling by decree. He is accustomed to issuing commands. Having a third-party facilitator on board can help to draw out the others. The facilitator can interject questions or directly ask them for their perspectives. If they feel excluded from meaningful conversation, resentments are bound to build.

More often than not, having financial affluence can magnify family dysfunction. A wealthy family could risk a fortune if the children get steamrolled and never learn what it takes to manage finances appropriately. People often tell me that they worry more about their children's ability to handle an inheritance or take over a business than their own financial security. Family meetings are a prime opportunity to teach the next generation the values that went into building the wealth rather than where and how much the valuables are worth in dollar terms. How else will they learn the principles that their parents or grandparents took to heart?

The parents, however, should be careful what they communicate about money to their children. We all carry with us some impression from early in life about the meaning of money. Some are taught that money establishes their significance and stature. They measure their importance by the size of their portfolios. Money is a limited resource, some believe, particularly if they have known hard times. Others who have observed the power of investment, see money as an expandable resource. For some, making a lot of money is the answer to life's problems. For others, it's the source of life's problems. Some fear losing what they have, while others believe that what they have is never enough. A dysfunctional attitude doesn't necessarily inhibit the accumulation of wealth, but it often inhibits peace and happiness in the family.

When the parents can honestly evaluate their core beliefs about money, they can assess whether their attitude will help the children or hinder them. To insist that the kids focus on the pursuit of money could quell a passion in them that ultimately would be even more lucrative simply because they would be doing something they love. Autocratic parents who won't listen to their children's views might be sacrificing the spirit of innovation and creativity that builds a truly thriving self-confident person to be the best version of themselves.

Without deeper core values and guiding principles, money loses meaning—and those values do not just pass on by osmosis. The children need to hear the passion and commitment in their parents' voices. Whenever the parents communicate the wrong thing, or nothing at all, the result is the loss of potential that could do so much for oneself and for others. If their parents hoard money, or revel in possessions, the children are likely to do the same. We reveal our hearts by the things we treasure—and our children are watching.

# Sharing the Family Stories

When family members convene regularly and truly listen to one another, they tune in to the heritage that has made them who they are. Family pride develops as they share the stories handed down from previous generations. Those stories may be funny or profound—and sometimes, they are not very pretty. Some stories may teach lessons, and others will be just silly, but together, they communicate that each member of the family is part of the flow. They communicate a sense of belonging to something bigger than oneself. The stories reinforce the family's foundation.

So often people wish that they had asked their elders more about the family roots while they had the chance. That shared culture should be part of the family wealth, as worthy of handing down as any amount of money. Often, the stories tell of sacrifice and passions and of dreams fulfilled or deferred. They are a collage of struggles and successes, of laughter and pain, of victories and regrets. Young people need to understand what happened in the past so that they can learn from it and either emulate it or choose to build something stronger.

When those stories illustrate the core values that guided a family to success, they are indispensable.

Such has been the case in our family. My mother, Jane, insisted on our togetherness—because she knew from sad experience the pain of separation. Growing up in Hawaii, she had two older sisters and two younger brothers. When she was about age ten, her mother left the family, taking with her only the youngest boy, who was still an infant.

My grandfather, a Filipino immigrant, did his best to provide for the other four with what he could earn as a laborer in the pineapple fields. As a little girl, my mother spent much of her time cooking and cleaning for the family and caring for her younger brother, George. It was a tender age for such responsibilities.

Meanwhile, as the years passed, the infant boy who had been the youngest in our family became the oldest in another family after my grandmother remarried and had more children. His name was Ernest, and one day, when he was of high school age, he went to the drag races. There he saw a car with "Rapera and Son" in bold letters on its sides—my grandfather and his older son, George, had taken up racing as a hobby. Ernest recognized the name of his biological father, whom he had never met, having grown up on the other side of the island. During a break in the races, Ernest approached the two men as they were tinkering with the race car.

"My name is Ernest, and, well, I think I might be your son," the teenager told my grandfather. And turning to the younger man, just a few years older than himself, he said: "And I'm wondering if you're my big brother?"

And that's how my Uncle Ernest was reunited with our side of the family—and how my mom and her siblings were reunited with the woman who had left them so many years before. Uncle Ernest became the bridge between the two families. He tried to bring everyone into fellowship, as best as he was able.

My mother tried, too, but she struggled. She felt, however, that she at least should introduce us to her birth mother. One day when I was about seven years old, she pulled my brother and me aside. "In a few minutes, you're going to meet a lady," she said, "and it's the woman who gave birth to me."

"We're going to meet your mom?" I said. "We're going to meet our grandma?"

"No. She's not my mom," she said, sternly. Seeing that my brother and I were bewildered, she told us that a true mom is always there for her children and does not leave them. "I just want you to meet her—but don't call her Grandma," she warned us. "Don't bring it up at all."

We then were ushered into a room where the sort-of-grandmother approached us with a tentative smile. Still trying to make sense of the situation, I popped out what seemed to me to be the obvious question to ask her: "So why did you leave my mom?" Her smile slowly faded, and she turned and walked to the window to gaze at something far away dodging my question. Almost immediately, I felt my mom's grip on my arm.

Nobody talked about "abandonment issues" in those days, but no doubt that is what my mom was dealing with into her adulthood. Her childhood pain, however, did not paralyze her. It motivated her to do differently for her own family. She was determined to be the mom for us that her own mom never was. She drilled into us the importance of family—a value that already was deep within the heart of the man she had married.

Most families can recount heartaches of the past, but they should not define us. My mom made it clear to us that she had made a choice to overcome those heartaches and not recycle them. She would not allow that early feeling of abandonment to diminish her confidence and her sense of self-worth. She lived a life of resolve, not of regrets.

A devout Catholic Christian, my mother's faith sustained her. It was her father who shaped her religious beliefs; her mother, whose family had come from Japan, had been raised Buddhist. My mom understood that God puts challenges in our path that ultimately strengthen who we are to become.

At Apriem Advisors, we serve many multigenerational families from a variety of backgrounds, some similar to mine and some very different, yet we often share the same assortment of life's concerns. Our emphasis for all of them, as we assist with their financial planning, is that clear values and family unity are essential if the money is to have any enduring meaning. That emphasis is rooted in my own upbringing and what I learned from my parents' example.

We must tell our stories, both the good ones and the sad ones, and learn from them. If you feel your family life is a mess, take heart. So many people feel the same way. Brokenness is the human condition—but I have seen, over and over, how new beginnings can arise from dysfunctions. If you think you should wait until your family gets its act together before convening a family meeting, you may be waiting longer than you think. It's never too late to start the conversations.

# TWO IMPORTANT QUESTIONS

Family relationships are the ultimate investment. Successful families come to realize that they must focus first on building those relationships and identifying the values that unite them. They prioritize love over money. Still, the sad truth is that love of money can often take precedence over the love of the family. Financial decisions certainly have an important place in family discussions, but without financial wisdom, those decisions will lack substance.

That wisdom develops as loved ones gather at the table to clarify their values and give money a purpose. The family leaders need to take care not to send mixed signals. "We want our children to learn the value of hard work," they often will tell me. Then, as we talk about how much of an inheritance the children should get, the parents often say that they want them to have enough to be comfortable.

"Oh, you mean so they won't have to work anymore?" I ask. I can see the recognition registering on their faces as they grapple with the irony: *How does one encourage a strong work ethic in the kids while also arranging for them to get by without working?*

And what will the kids consider to be "comfortable" life, anyway? A cabin in the woods where they can enjoy solitude without the clutter of possessions? Or a house with five bedrooms and an ocean view? How will they prefer to spend their time? Riding their bike around the neighborhood? Or will they feel uncomfortable unless they have enough money for a luxury trip around the world? Ask ten people to define comfortable, and you will get ten different answers. What is comfortable for some is intolerable for others. Contentment is not measured by how much money you have. It is measured by how much you think you need. Discontent arises from wanting what you don't have—and for some people, more will not be enough.

I often hear parents emphasizing a top-notch education for the kids. Why? "So they can get a good job and earn a great income." But a good education in itself cannot be just about getting a good job and earning a great income, especially if the kids know that they will be living great on a multimillion-dollar trust fund and a large inheritance. The goal of studying hard to secure a lucrative job will not be an easy sell to a young person whose family owns several houses and regularly vacations in five-star exotic places. Instead, the family will need to emphasize that the pursuit of higher education is a value independent of monetary gain. It is an enrichment measured not in dollars but in knowledge and wisdom.

Every family, and the individuals within, should ponder two questions that help to identify the driving values for their financial decisions. First: *If you had one day left to live, what would you do and say to those you care most about?*

Imagine yourself possessing the knowledge that in twenty-four hours you will die. You have two young children. What will you say to them? What will you say to your spouse? How will you spend that time? I'm thinking you wouldn't be checking on how the stock market did that day. It is more likely that you would be offering comfort to your loved ones and sharing the truths and values that you would want them to cherish as a remembrance of who you were to them. And you will likely want to spend your last precious twenty-four hours with them.

Once you can answer that question, then ask yourself the second question: *If money were not an issue, what would you do with your life?* By temporarily removing money from the equation, you move from the practical to the passionate. That will help you discover a vision and a mission for yourself and your family.

Life is precious, and death is certain. None of us, neither wealthy nor poor, will be carrying a penny with us when we die. In many families, the inherited money goes whichever way the wind blows, and in a generation or two, it is gone. You can do better. If you have been blessed with wealth, you can designate it to accomplish something great, to create a legacy of your choosing. Long after you are gone, your money can continue to serve a purpose that you and your family assigned to it.

# In the Spirit of Kokua

Growing up in a household where our friends often gathered, I heard my father frequently use the Hawaiian word *kokua* when requesting or offering a helping hand. Kokua is not just any kind of help, though. In the Hawaiian culture, it is sacrificial assistance with no expectation of personal gain. In the spirit of kokua, one pitches in cooperatively with kindness and consideration.

My upbringing was rooted in the island's aloha traditions—the kokua value of selfless service, the ohana value of treating everyone like family—and I was also reinforced by the Christian faith my parents embraced. As my own faith grew, I understood that those concepts are not just a Hawaiian island thing but also a God thing. To love our neighbors as ourselves is the greatest commandment in life. To love others is to serve others, and to serve others, you have to be in relationship with others, offering your time, your talents, and often your treasures.

Fundamentally our family vision is about building relationships and serving people. Serving people, however, is a universal value not restricted to any particular religion. In one way or another, every family's vision and mission will be about people and how to make life more fulfilling for your family and others, whether by feeding the needy or by supporting the arts and sciences. Reaching out to others—in the home, the community, the world—is an admirable quality of our human nature, and that can be expressed in countless ways.

That commitment requires planning. When loved ones gather at the table for the family meeting, they can express the heart, mind, and soul of what it means to be a family. Once they start talking, they can discover a more significant purpose. They can establish their guiding values—and then use wealth as a tool to support those values in specific ways. They will realize that their wealth does not define them. Their values define them. Their self-worth is independent of their net worth.

Around the table, the children can learn the meaning of money and how to use it wisely, in keeping with the family mission. Unless the parents teach the next generation well, the wealth is unlikely to last long, and no one will know what might have been. By passing on an abundance of wisdom along with wealth, the parents can keep the family's good fortunes intact to serve generations to come.

# CHAPTER 4

# Redefining Financial Freedom

———————

Frank was a bully. He might have been a bully since his days on the playground, for all I know. Though he was a big success at building a business, his family life was a mess. He tried to manipulate and control his wife and children. He would demand that his wife sign documents while insisting that she did not need to read them. His style as a dad was to issue one demand after another, expecting immediate and unquestioning compliance, convinced that he was showing strength of leadership. He dangled his wealth in front of his kids, telling them that they would not get a cent of inheritance unless they met his overbearing expectations. He berated them and tried to make them feel insignificant. He treated his wife with disrespect and made sure everyone knew he was in charge.

The high cost of Frank's approach was the disintegration of his family and the relationships within it. His wife divorced him.

Some of the kids sided with Mom and some with Dad. Some of the siblings did not speak to one another, or to their father, for years. The wife did well without him. Once released, she felt a sense of liberation and empowerment.

As for Frank, I suspect that unless he got help, he has not changed. He had his pile of money—and that is often the big problem. Sometimes, people who have achieved great financial success can count up their millions and say, "Hey, it worked for me, and this is my reward. I'm doing everything right." True, bullies often manage to get their way, and they can be as savvy as anyone else. Sometimes, they can rake together a fortune, just as a demeaning but demanding coach can add a trophy to the shelf. But they achieve insignificant success. People who try to justify their blustering behavior by pointing out the results are simply not seeing all the results. They are deluding themselves. They have lost any semblance of harmony in their lives.

Even if he had been destitute, Frank likely would have been an abuser anyway. The emotional games that he played emanated from somewhere deep within. Bullies often were bullied themselves and are driven by insecurities. They are out to show the world that they are not the nobodies that someone kept telling them they were. But whatever Frank's character issues, his money became another way to display them. He felt that wealth granted him the freedom to act as he pleased. In truth, he was trapped in his own little world of me, myself, and I.

Money often magnifies what is already in the heart. In the wrong hands, it can be a tool to manipulate others and jockey for power. Having lots of money does not make a person greedy. Greed already existed before the money arrived. Without basic, decent values firmly in place, money can splinter families. The problem is not the money, which can be a force for so much good. The problem is in the heart of our values. Our personality traits, like our finances, often get handed down to the next generations. While the money comes and goes, the behavioral flaws tend to persist—and it is the latter that often causes the former.

It's more worthwhile to pass down the virtues that reside in the core of our humanity. Where there is dysfunction, we must make an effort to disrupt the cycle. This is the way to achieve and preserve what I call healthy wealth. The path to financial freedom does not come from amassing great wealth, as Frank seemed to believe. It comes instead when you reach the understanding where you are deliberately using your assets to enhance the well-being of others. Otherwise, having more just for the sake of having more becomes pointless.

"It was so much easier when we didn't have much money," people often have told me, reminiscing about when life was simple. A widespread assumption is that greater wealth solves life's problems. It doesn't. It can add to them. People fall victim to the belief that they will find freedom from worry by working endless hours and enduring life-shortening stress. They end up feeling more worry and stress than ever. Our culture promotes the "work, work, work" ethic beyond the point where it is healthy. It is amazing what people will do for money. We have often confused the busy life as the good life. When we're asked, "how are you doing," we typically say, "I am good, but busy" as if that is a response that things really are good. Are we good?

Positive financial decision-making starts with understanding oneself and being true to a strong sense of values. Many people struggle to break free of patterns that developed early in life and that have been holding them back from the life they dream about. Recognition is the first step to overcoming those behavioral handicaps—and that awareness comes from a willingness to be open and vulnerable with loved ones in an encouraging and nurturing atmosphere. It comes from learning to listen and a willingness to change. Those who finally see the potential in themselves can begin to see a greater potential for their assets. They are on the right path to financial freedom.

# THE TRUTH IS...

Our society suffers from an epidemic of financial dysfunction. It's not that good financial management is rocket science but rather our behavioral issues so often get in the way. There are really only three things you can do with your money once you pay your taxes and your debts. You can spend it, save it, or give it away. The simple truth to success in personal finances is this: Spend less than you earn, save for a rainy day, and avoid excessive debt. So, you don't need to have an advanced degree in finance to understand this truth. Like most things, good behavior is paramount to desired results.

Americans certainly are fond of spending. Our culture consistently has had one of the lowest savings rates, and consumer debt drags people down. They tend to think short-term, unwilling to defer gratification. Many regularly spend all they make, and more, living as if tomorrow will never come. *It's pointless to save for retirement*, they tell themselves. *What if I don't even make it to sixty-five?* To which I say: What if you do? And what if you make it to seventy-five or ninety-five?

## AVERAGE RETIREMENT SAVINGS BALANCE BY AGE

| Age Group | Average Retirement Savings Balance Amount ($) |
|---|---|
| Under 35 | 49,130 |
| 35–44 | 141,520 |
| 45–54 | 313,220 |
| 55–64 | 537,560 |
| 65–74 | 609,230 |

*Based on data from the 2022 Survey of Consumer Finances, Source: Federal Reserve Board*

## MEDIAN RETIREMENT SAVINGS BALANCE BY AGE

| Age Group | Median Retirement Savings Balance Amount ($) |
|---|---|
| Under 35 | 18,880 |
| 35–44 | 45,000 |
| 45–54 | 115,000 |
| 55–64 | 185,000 |
| 65–74 | 200,000 |

*Based on data from the 2022 Survey of Consumer Finances, Source: Federal Reserve Board*

You could hire the world's best financial planner and get the same advice that common sense should dictate: If you spend more than you earn, you will end up with less than nothing. You can turn that situation around by paying what you owe and saving for the future. Nothing complicated about that—and yet people nonetheless take on massive debt. They willingly step on the treadmill. Once, the treadmill was a device used in debtors' prisons on which inmates would be ordered to labor for hours to no avail. Working to exhaustion with nothing to show for it was considered the ultimate punishment. Today, people willingly subject themselves to something similar.

I am not saying all debt is bad. Consumer debt is bad, yes. Credit cards pick your pocket at ghastly interest rates. Smart investors, though, often have used debt as leverage. They borrow money to purchase assets, such as real estate, that have a promising potential to increase in value. Other investors buy stocks on margin with the expectation that those stocks will show gains. Doing so requires careful calculation and insight, however, to avoid the nightmare of the asset losing value, as many have experienced. Student debt might be considered an investment in the future, except that it puts so many young people in a financial bind right at the outset of their careers as they are trying to start a family—or else Mom and Dad sacrifice their ability to retire comfortably in order to bankroll an expensive college education for the kids. Still, some kinds of debt can be good if acquired selectively and wisely for financial growth.

Unfortunately, for many people, debt is nothing but a big financial drain. They lack a clear plan for how they will pay it back and whether they can afford to do so. What borrowers often fail to realize is that they will be paying more than the interest and principal, which alone can be onerous. They do not stop to think that they will be paying back the loan with after tax earnings. In other words, someone in a 25 percent tax bracket who borrows $10,000 will need to earn $13,333 to produce enough net income to pay it all back. Companies make the same mistake as individuals that way, creating serious cash flow issues.

Nobody should accept debt without a plan to pay it back and the confidence that they can afford the payments. Otherwise, stay away from it. A lot of people know what they should do, but they don't do it, just as they often fail to take the advice of the doctor who prescribes exercise and a balanced diet as the best way to stay in good health. "Sure, thanks, doc," they say but continue lounging in front of the

TV and munching potato chips. They would prefer to think that they could swallow some magic pill if their health took a bad turn. The same attitude often hurts people's financial wellness. There really is no shortcut to the truth. Don't expect the lotto to bail you out. Don't figure that you can just rack up another credit card.

At Apriem, we approach achieving financial security a little different. Rather than trying to figure out a budget with each expense line itemed monthly and annually, we focus on what percentage or a specific amount of money you need to save and invest in order to achieve the future lifestyle you desire. The word budget often sends chills down spines. Budgets can be very difficult to establish and to adhere too. I have met very few people who can stick to one with consistency. Our general advice on this matter is to focus more on what you're able to save than what you are spending.

## When Financial Security Falls Short

Cynthia and Harold did not consider themselves wealthy. They lived well within their means on his salary as a university professor. They raised one daughter who was able to get a good education. The couple had more money than they needed, though they seemed unaware of that fact. Through the years, they continued to live modestly.

As the couple got older, they had plenty of money coming in from pension plans and returns on their portfolio, yet they still did not feel financially secure. I tried to reassure them, but no matter how many times I said, "You're going to be okay," they were less than convinced. Harold increasingly was struggling and eventually was diagnosed with Alzheimer's disease. He was admitted to a care facility, where the costs started rising to thousands of dollars a month.

Cynthia was worried. "Can I afford this?" she asked me. I showed her that they had sufficient assets to afford the best of care for Harold, and that is what he received until he passed away. The whole time, though, Cynthia fretted over the finances—and when she became a widow, she still needed those frequent reminders that she would be all right. She had an inheritance coming, and I sat down with her and showed her the figures.

"Cynthia, have you considered what you want to do with all this? You have plenty for yourself and your own needs, so what about the rest? How might you make a difference in the world with this wealth that Harold and you put together through such wise decisions over the years?"

"Well, we've always thought that we would like to do more to help others," she said, and after a little questioning, she began to talk about her passion for some organizations and causes that she would like to support—if she only had the money.

"The thing is, Cynthia, you *do* have the money," I told her. She still was not sure about that. Cynthia began donating to various charities every year, but regularly, she would ask the same question: "Can I afford to be doing this?" Our staff did a financial model for her that demonstrated how much she could donate and still be financially secure, and the amount surprised her. She began giving away $100,000 a year, and sometimes, more.

I witnessed Cynthia's transformation from financial security to financial freedom. When I met her and Harold, they were secure even though neither really grasped that fact. They had the money they needed for the lifestyle they wanted—and that's financial security. It took years, though, for Cynthia to move beyond security and attain the peace of mind that characterizes financial freedom. She knew that she had enough. She knew that their daughter had enough, even without the inheritance she would be receiving. That knowledge gave her confidence—and that confidence finally released her from worry so that she could reach outward, pursuing a purpose. She became one of the most joyful people I have known.

Financial freedom is an elusive concept. Many who think that they are pursuing it instead are losing it. They spend years building their assets but never feel confident that they have enough. They want freedom, which they equate with security—whatever that might be. They don't know. It is not a matter of one's chosen lifestyle. Some people, like Harold and Cynthia, live frugally and save prudently. Others live large, in a relentless quest to earn more and more so they can spend more and more. The tower is never quite high enough. In either case, what stands in the way of financial freedom is worry—the fear that the money will run short.

In the course of my career, I have met many wealthy people who still worry that they won't have enough money. In time, they often come to see that money isn't enough. They remain burdened by stress, and they feel aimless. Something is missing.

Their fears are many. What if their investments turn south and they lose their life's savings? What if they entrust their wealth to the wrong person who siphons it away? What if someone sues them? Will the kids be able to handle their inheritance—and what if any of them divorces? Will the surviving spouse know what to do and make the right decisions? What if their health fails and they need to spend years in long-term care? And what about all those taxes? Those are just a few of their worries. Yes, those are real concerns, all of them. And there are solutions and safeguards for all of them.

So many people put a priority on reaching financial security, and they never really feel that they have arrived. They never find that peace of mind. Life can be much more fulfilling when the priority is on identifying a purpose, a reason for being. Finding a vision and mission for your family might require a lot of painstaking soul-searching, but it's the antidote to aimlessness and boredom. It's an investment in true financial freedom—and like any investment, the sooner you get started, the greater it can grow.

It comes down to being prepared for what comes along in life. The more money people have, the more complex their concerns can become—until they take the right steps to resolve them and release themselves from that bondage. A wealth advisor can help by providing a clear financial picture and assisting in getting in place the pieces to the puzzle that address all those worries. Seeing the big picture is what it takes to move from security to freedom.

You do need sufficient resources, of course. I suppose it is possible to be financially free without any income, like some happy hobo, but that more likely would be a state of denial. Typically, I encounter people who simply do not know whether they have enough or how much that might be. They live in uncertainty, without peace of mind. Their wealth is sufficient to more than meet their needs and desires, so making more money will not improve their lives or make them happier. Once they recognize that truth, their eyes open to the needs of others. They reach the point where they can look outward instead of just inward—and that is the liberating moment when they have reached financial freedom.

## What Matters Most?

Each of us will leave this world with what we had when we came, which is nothing. Naked we arrived, Scripture tells us, and naked we will depart. We will leave behind whatever resources we have assembled in a lifetime that we did not use ourselves for basic needs of food, shelter, and clothing and for whatever extras we desired. Once we feel confident that we can meet those needs and desires, we then can start thinking about what to do with whatever amount that we cannot take with us at the final farewell.

Many people want to leave some portion to their children, to help them build their financial security—and then, the question becomes how much is too much. If the family relationships are solid and the children have developed financial wisdom based on meaningful values, the assets should be in good hands as the family legacy extends to the next generation and beyond. All too often, however, the money damages relationships rather than enhancing them—as in the case of the overbearing dad who sought to control his family on the pretext of providing for them. Somehow young people never seem to respond well to the sentiment of "I did all this for you, so be grateful, and the least you could do for me is such-and-such." The money should be a tool for building healthy relationships. It should not be used as a carrot or a stick. A big inheritance can cause big trouble—and that is why some parents instead choose to leave much or all their assets to charity.

For every family, the decisions are different—but it comes down to answering the question of what you hope to accomplish by achieving financial success. You need an answer to the "why"—and making more money for its own sake is not a good enough reason. You could have the largest portfolio in town, but what then? You could collect properties and wheel and deal, as if life were some big Monopoly game, but still feel empty if all you are doing is going round and round, endlessly passing "Go" without collecting much of enduring worth. Sure, it might feel good to keep up with the Joneses. And it's great to know you can pay all the bills—but once you drill down to the true "why," you might see that what drives you is providing safety and security for your family.

Our values influence not only how we spend our money but how we spend our time. What will we do in pursuit of our dreams and hopes? Each of us is uniquely equipped to do more than simply stockpile.

The question resonates through eternity: *Why are you here?* What will be your legacy? The possibilities of who might benefit from your life's work are nearly endless, but the choices must align with personal values. That is why I put so much emphasis on the importance of family meetings. Discovering those values together is an essential step in the ascent to financial security with peace of mind.

In the end, that togetherness is a family's greatest asset. Working in unity to accomplish a clear purpose, each family can contribute to a powerful force for change in our society. And though those discussions must include how to make the best use of the resources, the togetherness arises not from the family finances but from the family's shared passions. When the spirit of "this is who we are" pervades the conversations, it drives away the selfishness and pettiness that can wreck relationships.

Think back to a fond childhood memory that has stayed with you through the years. Even if your family, like so many, was entrenched in turmoil, you probably hold on to some precious moments. Did money play much of a role? Or was it something else that gave you joy, or comfort, or hope, or even a moment of relief? When I was a boy, I cherished our family camping trips. Our tent was finer than any five-star hotel. The woods were better than any amusement park. I can still hear those voices around the campfire. We were together.

I recently asked Troy, one of our twin sons, to recall a fond moment from his childhood. He came up with a memory two decades old. "Learning to ride my bike without training wheels," he said, "that time we went camping at Sequoia National Park." At nineteen dollars a night, that was hardly a lavish vacation, but he was recalling something priceless. Fancy vacations are fine, sure, but when you get down to the simple truth, most of us feel a deep human longing for connection. We want to touch hearts with others, to know and to be known.

"Money can't buy happiness" is an old saying for good reason. It's true. More money doesn't automatically translate to financial security or financial peace of mind. It's really not a matter of how much you earn or how much you have but rather how you can build your life within your means, enjoying life in the process. When you can do that, you have financial freedom—and it lies at the confluence of security, peace of mind, and purpose.

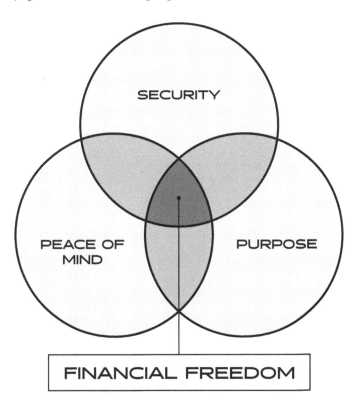

I care about money, but I care mostly about people—and how money, when used wisely, can make their lives better. When a family can rally its resources effectively to attain financial security for itself, the doors then can open to doing so much more to build connections and relationships in the broader family of humanity. That can come through a gesture as grand as endowing a scholarship or as simple as wiping away a tear.

Good financial decision-making does not come naturally, and stewarding significant wealth can be very challenging indeed. Yet, for the sake of our own self-care, our families, and others, we have a responsibility to do our very best. And the only way to achieve that is by having open conversations with your family about finances. In the next chapter, I'll discuss how I approach these discussions in my own family.

# CHAPTER 5

# Significance Beyond Success

---

Our daughter Haley came home from her first year at Baylor University with a couple of questions for me.

"Dad, when I explain to people that I'm studying social work," she said, "I get two responses. Some of them say, 'Wow, that's a tough field, you're going to see some really difficult stuff.' Or they respond, 'The world needs people like you, but you're not going to make a lot of money.'"

I looked into her eyes and waited to hear how she felt about that. "It makes me wonder," she said. "Should I study something that is easy and helps me earn a lot of money?"

"No, Haley, that's not what it's all about," I said, reminding her of the importance of following one's passions.

"Oh, I see, Dad," she said with a smile. "So I don't need to be thinking about doing something like what *you* do, then, right?"

My daughter was having some fun with me, and I could tell that she didn't really need my advice on that matter. She had long since learned that if you put your heart into what you do, not only will you do well at it, but you will also achieve significance. It's a shame to spend years doing something you don't like for the sake of money. What matters most is not what you can get but rather the impact you have on others by what you can give.

I was relieved to see that I had not somehow led our children to think that money is everything. It certainly is significant, but only in its proper place. The highest significance rests in the values that we impart to the next generation, not the valuables we leave behind. Those values are what define our legacy.

## Unity over Uniformity

While our four children were still young adults of college and high school age, we decided it was time to call them together for a different kind of family meeting. This one was more formal than our typical chats around the dinner table. To underscore the serious tone of the conversation, we gathered in the conference room of my friend Sam's private equity firm. They were old enough now to contemplate some life-and-death matters.

Much of the conversation was practical. We shared a lot more details of our family finances, charitable giving, and estate planning documents, on which we recently had named the children as successor trustees. Previously, we had designated an outside trustee to act on their behalf if something were to happen to Lea and me.

Talking about the prospect of dying is difficult, but the topic must be addressed. In the spirit of unity, the conversation should emphasize the "why" that governs family decisions. I started with this scenario: "What if your mom and I went on a trip and the plane crashed and you didn't have us anymore? What then?"

My intent in asking such a startling question was to make sure that their heads were not buried in the sand. Tragedy can strike anyone at any time, regardless of who you are, where you live, or whether you are rich or poor. Nobody should scare little kids with such stories, of course, but all parents should make sure that their big kids, at the appropriate stage of maturity, have a clear perspective on life and loss. I highly recommend working with an estate planning attorney to draft legal documents such as wills, trusts, powers of attorney, and health directives. Such preparation helps immensely in a time of grief.

At our meeting, I wanted to express that life is fragile and that tomorrow is not promised to any of us. Throughout our children's childhood, we had expressed to them that every day was precious and that we should count every moment together as irreplaceable. Now, it was time to reinforce that value of unity with some practical examples. "If the day comes when your mom and dad are gone," I told them, "our greatest hope for you is unity. We want to know that you will carry on without us and never let money or anything or anyone else come between you." After all, our greatest disappointment would be broken relationships between our children and their respective families.

I have seen families torn apart because feelings get hurt over something that, in the long run, should be inconsequential. Families should learn to cooperate and communicate and make concessions. We can overcome our weaknesses by being one another's strength. "Pity anyone who falls," says Scripture, "and has no one to help them up" (Ecclesiastes 4:10). Loved ones must speak the truth in love to each other, sharpening each other as iron sharpens iron.

That's what family is all about. If you cannot reach out to others within your family, how can you expect to do so outside your family?

We wanted our children to stand together, like the braided cord that is stronger than the sum of its strands. We called them together to emphasize that their relationships with one another was their greatest treasure, something to cherish and protect.

## Is Equal the Same as Fair?

"Do you think that your mother and I have made decisions that were unfair to any of you?" I asked our children during that meeting. They assured us that we had been fair in their estimation.

"What if I were to tell you that we have not been fair—and that we wanted it that way?"

Puzzled looks came my way from all round the table.

"Well, it's true, we weren't always fair," I said. "That is, not if 'fair' means treating you all equal." I looked at our daughter. "Haley, what sport were you in, all through high school?"

"Cheer," she said. "Competitive cheerleading."

"And was that an expensive sport?"

"Sure, because of all the travel and uniforms and private coaching and all that."

I turned to the boys. "And you guys were in track and field, which cost, what, maybe a few hundred dollars and a couple pairs of shoes and spikes? That was a fraction of what we paid for Haley. Do you feel disadvantaged because of that?"

"Heck no, Dad," the boys said, almost in unison.

"Okay, we just wanted to be sure," I said. "Because we don't want you thinking someday that your parents played favorites just because they spent more money on one than on another." They assured us again that they had no problem with our decisions.

"It's important to understand that equal isn't the same thing as fair," I said, driving home the point. "Life isn't about everything being 50/50." I looked at Lea and smiled. "And I know it's not that way in marriage. Sometimes your mom has given 99 percent to lift me up when I needed it, and I'd do the same for her."

Then, I asked our children to close their eyes and flash forward in time. "Imagine now that your mom and I are gone, and you're all married with kids, nice homes, good jobs. We have a plan set up for the benefit of your families, but you all are doing well without it."

"Now, suppose that one of you is facing a big challenge. You have a child with chronic medical problems that are extremely expensive. You're struggling with all those bills, and you can't seem to focus at work. Life has become very stressful."

I looked around the table. "So what do you think? If that's you, would you consider it fair to get a special provision from the family funds because you need it and the others don't?" After a long pause, I said, "Let me put it this way. If we were still alive when that happened, what do you think we'd do? Would you all get an equal share?"

"Probably not...," one of them ventured. "You'd take a lot of things into consideration." The others nodded.

"And there's your answer," I said. "You know, sometimes it's not *one for you, one for me; two for you, two for me*. Sometimes, it's *two for you, one for me*. Sometimes, it's *none for me*."

"In an ideal world, 'fair' might mean everyone gets an equal share," I continued. "But it's not always an ideal world. There is a difference between doing what appears to be right versus doing what is good for the sake of each other, and for the sake of the relationship. These are the kind of decisions that come up in every family, and we hope this is the way you'll approach some of life's more difficult financial decisions."

When people begin to take that approach within their families, they tend to broaden that thinking to the wider world. Our American freedom is unknown in much of the world. We can make of it what we will.

Money cannot buy values, but it is a great way to express them—and when those values are passed to the children, they receive a far more rewarding and enduring inheritance than the sum and total of a family's valuables. They don't just get money. They get real purpose from what money means to the family and to others in the circle of influence. Instead of fighting for our fair share, we have the opportunity to use our money to bring families together.

# What Is Success?

"The future is in computers!" I often heard back in high school. "You'll make a lot of money if you get into that." In college, I took a few computer and programming classes but soon discovered that I hated them—so I changed direction to focus on finances, which fascinated me. Sure, I wanted to do well, but making money is only a fraction of the equation that equals success.

Each of us is uniquely designed to contribute in his or her own way to a better world. I have met a lot of people who have spent years plugging along in a stagnant career without enthusiasm or initiative. They feel little motivation to excel, and often that is because they settled for what others told them they should do rather than learning to discover if there is a field or career they are truly called to.

Even after beginning my career in finance, I realized that I still was on the wrong path. My corporate job was not a bad start, but it was not where I wanted to end up. I was not cut out for high-pressure sales. I discovered that I enjoyed providing good client experience through service.

If I have succeeded in instilling our family values in our children, they in turn will be encouraging their own kids to dig down deep to discover what drives them to do things. Service to others is one of our principal family values. From an early age, our children all learned the discipline of serving, and I believe that has translated into the careers that they are developing today. They understand that success is not measured by the size of a paycheck or by the size of a house.

Some parents communicate, either directly or by example, that those material goals matter most, and their children spend decades trying to prove themselves—until the day when they recognize that keeping up with the Joneses gets mighty expensive and exhausting. The children begin to wonder whether Mom and Dad valued the Joneses more than them. The problem often is that "success" was never defined, and so the children lean on what they have observed, allowing others and culture to define success for them. The beginning must always start with an end in mind; otherwise, we are destined to repeat the mistakes again and again.

In my family, we have tried to communicate that success comes from pursuing a passion. That's what drives excellence. As parents, we engaged our children in conversations on discovering those passions. The big question is: *What can I do to serve others by making the most of how God wired me?* To my father, service meant teaching. He wasn't in it for the money. Nor was I looking to make a lot of money when I became a financial advisor and started my own company. I wanted to serve. My dad and I both desired to help others fulfill the life they dreamed for themselves and their families by using our passion to help others.

As I write this, we have seen that emphasis on service taking root in each of our children. Our oldest son, Tyler, became an Air Force pilot, eager to serve his country. Haley received her master's in social work and is serving others as a mental health therapist. They both enjoy their careers and certainly did not choose their careers based on income potential. Troy and Kyle, our youngest two, likewise are exploring how they can contribute their natural talents as they reach to find their passions and significance.

My success will not be my children's. They will find their own way. Parents can best help their children along that path by paying attention to them. Only by listening to them and getting to truly know them can a parent help them to recognize and develop their unique gifts. Mom and Dad should guide their children on their journey of discovery, but they must take care not to discourage what God already has put into their hearts. He may have designed them to build empires for his purposes, or he may simply want them to offer comfort to people in need.

Either way, success is not about dollars. It's about the quest for significance. The measure of success is how we impact others, in ways big and small—not by what we do for ourselves.

## Crafting a Family Vision

One evening, when our twin boys were about seven years old, I heard a commotion and found them brawling in their room, their noses bleeding. I pulled them apart as they sputtered out their stories of who did what and who did it first. "Enough!" I shouted. "This doesn't happen in this house!"

As they sulked, I gathered my thoughts. *What can they learn from this?* I asked myself. It would do no good to just out-yell them. That would just teach them to out-yell others. I needed to act, not react. Lea and I had learned through experience not to let emotions get in the way when disciplining our children. "We'll talk tomorrow about how you're both going to make this right," I calmly told the boys. "Now get to bed!"

The next day, I sat them down at the kitchen table. "First, each of you is going to forgive each other, right now, right here." They mumbled out their apologies. "Okay, now each of you is going to write out for me what you did wrong," I continued. "Not what the other did wrong, what *you* did wrong." I gave them each a sheet of paper and told them what they wrote would go into their binders for our family meetings so that they would never forget what happened.

This was a defining moment as each of the boys recognized how he had contributed to a problem and then took responsibility to became part of the solution. All these years later, we still have those notes. A bad scene has become a cute memory. "I will never ever hurt my brother ever again," one of the boys wrote, and he drew stick figures depicting who had kicked whom.

*I will never hurt my brother*—and yet so often we do. We must forgive and move on. That does not necessarily come naturally in our world today, but it is the standard that we must embrace, inside our families and out. Family leaders set those standards for behavior, by word and deed.

Leadership flows from the top down, from confident individuals who can communicate their expectations decisively without domineering, allowing room for mistakes, learning, and growth. That is what it takes to build a strong company, and that is what it takes to build a strong family. And that is why it is as important for a family as it is for a business to clearly state a mission and a vision: *This is what we're all about, and this is where we are going.*

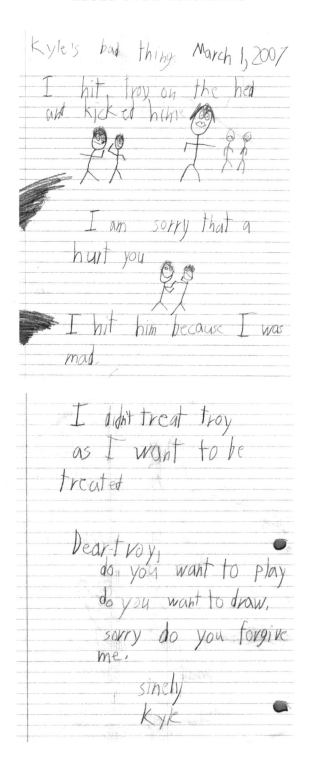

Kyle's bad thing    March 1, 2007

I hit troy on the hed
and kicked him

I am sorry that a
hurt you

I hit him because I was
mad.

I didn't treat troy
as I want to be
treated

Dear troy,
do you want to play
do you want to draw,
sorry do you forgive
me.
        sinely
        Kyle

98

Failure to instill the values for true success has generational consequences: Don't forget that old saying, "shirtsleeves to shirtsleeves in three generations." How soon the children can forget, if they ever knew, what it took to build something good. The wisdom of the elders is far more precious than gold, and they should run the family with at least as much care as they would run a business, with systems and expectations firmly in place.

"Harmon, how do you keep your family together?" a friend, Jerry, recently asked me. An executive at a major company, he was progressing well in his career, but he had become frustrated with a series of family issues.

"Well, for one thing, we hold family meetings," I told him. "We've been doing them pretty regularly since the kids were little. Have you ever considered calling your family together to talk about the things that matter most and to hear everybody out?"

"No, I've never..." Jerry looked thoughtful. "How do you go about getting started on doing that?"

"Try to find a time when you're all going to be together, like at dinnertime, and make sure to do a lot of listening and not just talking," I said. "You meet with people at work all the time, don't you?"

"Yeah we're always having meetings. That's how we stay on track with what we're all about. And we figure out where we're going next."

"Great!" I said. "So what would happen if you didn't bother to meet?"

"We'd all be going in different directions. Nobody would know what anyone was thinking, so it'd be hard to make much progress...." Jerry paused, then smiled. "I get what you're saying, Harmon. I call those office meetings to keep everybody together. So that's what I need to do in my home, too."

On the many lists of "best places to work," organizations are rated on a variety of criteria to determine their ranking. At those standout workplaces, the employees consistently comment that they enjoy their jobs. A decent paycheck and a generous benefit package matter, of course, but those are far from the only considerations. The employees want to stay because they feel valued. They are proud to contribute their skills and talents as productive members of a team that works cooperatively. They feel encouraged, not controlled, by leaders who clearly communicate their vision of what they want and how to make it happen. They are passionate about their work and about the people they serve. That passion drives their excellence.

Imagine a ranking for "best family to live in" and consider what such a family would look like. Some of the criteria would be like what you would find in an exemplary workplace. Everyone would feel valued as part of a team working cooperatively. The leaders would clearly communicate a vision and how to make it happen. They would define a purpose and set expectations, but their approach would be encouraging, not controlling.

A successful business develops a strong brand—a word that has come to mean not just the name of a product or service but also the values for which the company is known in the community. Smart business owners know that a respected brand is money in the bank. They communicate that brand clearly to all their employees, who are expected to reflect those values. A family's values are, in effect, its brand. The leadership's role is to communicate those values clearly to every member of the family, who should respect and uphold them, each in his or her own way.

For my family, I wanted a vision statement that would endure generationally. Getting it just right took a lot of work—but it also was a lot of work to develop such a statement for my company, and my family certainly was worth the effort. I understand how some family leaders feel overwhelmed at the prospect of so much brainstorming and soul-searching. Getting started matters most. I confess that I put off a formal family meeting for two years as I fine-tuned a vision statement, mission statement, and a list of family rules that we could take turns reading aloud at every meeting. In Appendix D, I've included our "Kong Ohana House Rules" as an example. My approach is one among many that families might follow, depending on what they consider most important in life.

Families often find that a vision is revealed to them along the way as they meet and talk about the issues that they are facing together. Family meetings are an opportunity for discovery—and what they discover might be startling. During those discussions, families often recognize their brokenness. They awaken from illusions of who they thought they were. I often have heard self-searching observations that start with *All this time...* or *I always thought...* or *Everyone always told me....* The family leaders confront that fundamental question, *why?*—and they cannot answer it. They lack a direction and a destination. What is their goal for the family? "I don't know," they say. "What outcomes are they expecting?" "I don't know." They see the disconcerting truth that they have been living without purpose. They are on their way to accomplishing what they have planned, which is nothing.

That revelation can be the motivation to address the deeper issues. If the family members are willing to make the necessary changes, they can fulfill a meaningful vision. By committing to making the effort rather than simply settling for whatever happens, they can turn things around dramatically, but they must start as soon as possible. By addressing dysfunction now, they can avoid the risk of paying dearly for it later as frustrations build into hostilities.

So, where to start? It helps to develop a list of guiding values and principles that the family can agree are important. Once those are articulated, it becomes easier to draft the vision and mission statements that reflect those principles. (See Appendix B for "Sample Family Vision and Mission Statements.") Those statements express the big goals. What is the family trying to do? What kind of adults will the children become? The family members then have a framework for their conversations and activities day by day. They can move forward with the end in mind. Together, they can celebrate their progress as they find themselves in alignment with the guidelines that they have agreed to embrace. It is hard to celebrate success when you do not know its definition.

# The Three Envelopes

When our children were little, we offered them a hard-to-resist incentive so that they would look forward to family meetings: That is when they got their allowance. Their allowance was not conditioned on proper behavior or completing chores. It was a given that they deserved the money; we were more interested in what they would do with it. Many parents do place such conditions on allowances, and that is fine when it fosters good discipline. Sometimes, it fosters something else. An overly controlling parent can turn allowances into a negative experience—"you've been *horrid*, so you get *nothing*!"—which could leave the child feeling apathetic with a "who cares, anyway?" attitude.

The message that we wished to impart to our children was: *This allowance money is yours simply because you are part of our family and as such you have privileges, but you must use it responsibly.* They each received an amount that was double their age. At age ten, for example, they got $20; at age eleven, $22. At first, that system elicited rumblings of *that's not fair!*

"Well, *fair* doesn't mean *equal*," I told them, instilling that lesson early. "As you get older, you'll be seeing that, over and over. That's the way life is. Just remember, the more you get, the more that's expected of you. You'll see that, too."

Each kid had three envelopes, labeled *spending, saving,* and *giving*. Whenever money came their way, whether from allowances or birthday gifts, they had to decide how to distribute it. "I'm never going to tell you how much you should put in each envelope," I told them, "but you shouldn't leave any of them empty."

That was our way of teaching them three basic principles of money. You can either spend it, save it, or give it away. (Paying taxes would be a later concept.) Fundamentally, those are the only three things that people can do with their money, and they should be figuring all three into their cash flow. I often have suggested to young families that they use the three-envelope system to begin teaching their children how to manage their money. The earlier that kids learn that they can do more with money than buy toys and candy, the better prepared they will be as adults to manage a family's finances.

I explained to our children that whatever they determined was spendable could come out of that envelope and go into their wallets. "You can use that spending money any way you want," I said, "so long as you are saving and giving, too." Their mom and I did offer appropriate guidance, as in: *Don't you think $40 is too much to stuff in your wallet all at once? What if you lose it?*

If they were saving up for something specific, they would write it on the saving envelope—a guitar, maybe, or bicycle, or computer game. "What you put in savings stays there," I explained. "Don't carry it around with you; that's what your spending money is for."

Their saving envelopes and contents had to remain untouched in their family meeting binders.

Their very first decision, however, had to be how much would go into their giving envelopes, which also stayed in their binders. How would they honor God with their generosity? Each kid could decide individually where to donate the money at the end of the year, or they could pool the money and decide collectively—and I would match that amount 100 percent. Each year, they chose to pool the money and donate it to a ministry that serves a poor community in the Philippines.

At Christmastime in 2005, our family traveled to the Philippines to visit Lea's mother. As a part of that trip, I also wanted our children to visit a community unlike ours so they can experience up close how much of the world does not live in the abundance to which we are accustomed. I had given them each a special allowance to spend on the trip. As we were chatting with family out on the patio in the evening, a group of local children stopped outside the gate and began singing Christmas songs and playing their instruments. They were going house to house, collecting a few coins here and there for their efforts.

When the singing stopped, Kyle, who was five years old, dodged into the house and returned with a fistful of money. It was everything he had for the trip, about forty dollars. Kyle ran up to the wrought-iron gate and reached through to drop the money into the hands of the singers, who were speechless. I gestured to them that it was all right to accept it.

"Kyle! What did you *do*?" his big brother Tyler exclaimed. "What were you *thinking*?" We all were astonished, which Kyle interpreted as disapproval—and fearing that he had done something wrong, his chin quivered as his eyes brimmed with tears.

"No, he's okay, leave him be," I told Tyler and knelt to wipe away Kyle's tears. "I'll tell you what you did, son," I said softly. "You gave from your heart, and God loves a cheerful giver."

I pulled out my wallet and counted out ten times what he had offered through the gate. "I can't multiply your gift thousands of times the way your heavenly father can, but I sure can show you how proud of you we are. This is yours, Kyle, and you can do with it what you wish." My son looked up at me, beaming, his weeping turning to joy, as somewhere down the street, the singing again filled the night air.

# CHAPTER 6

# Living Is Giving

---

Brad was a wealthy businessman who got that way by helping people get a start. "I never get tired of dealing with first-time home buyers," he told me. An Ivy-league architect, he chose to build a career specializing in affordable houses.

"The first-timers appreciate what we do, and it's all joy to them," he said. "You can see it in their faces. But when people are getting their second or third or fourth home—well, it's like they're thinking more about their warranty than how wonderful it is to have a house. I'd rather work with people who are excited to own their first home."

Brad found a passion in his work, and the family real estate construction business was flourishing. He didn't think of his family as wealthy, though. He and his wife, Bonnie, and their grown daughter were financially secure, and I pointed that out. "No doubt about it, you have more money than you need," I said. "Making more of it isn't going to improve or change your humble lifestyle. Congratulations, you have achieved financial security. So now what? Have you thought about what's next?"

"Well, sure, we're going to keep on doing what we enjoy," Brad said, "and running this business is still fun. It's not about making more money." With his expertise and talent, he could have been designing mansions, but he preferred to offer simple, attractive homes at an afford-able price. "There aren't enough houses that young families can buy," Bonnie explained. "We're proud to be doing something about that."

Recognizing that they had a beneficent bent, I suggested setting up a family foundation through which the three of them could choose charities to support. At first, they declined, maintaining that foun-dations were for folks with a level of wealth far greater than theirs. "We've got to put everything we can into growing this business by building more affordable housing." Braid said. "It's our baby. We have a lot of exciting ideas, but it's going to take money. We can't be just giving it away."

Three years later, though, they wanted to hear more. "That family foundation thing? It's time we did something as a family to give back," Bonnie told me. We worked out the details, and the couple sat down with their daughter to explore what mattered most to them. Soon they were contributing relief funds to victims of fires, hurricanes, and emergency response needs, donating to university endowments, and supporting faith-based organizations.

In my years as an advisor, I often have seen such journeys of gen-erosity as people conclude that life is about more than making money. For years, that family had done well by doing good, helping people of modest means attain the dream of home ownership. They made a lot of money for their efforts—and now they were relaxing their grip on those resources and reaching out to serve people who were pursuing a better life in other ways, or who were suffering setbacks along the way.

For Brad and Bonnie and their daughter, the big benefit came from identifying and expressing a sense of purpose that aligned with their family values. Yes, philanthropy certainly carries tax benefits, but neither that nor social prestige should be at the core of what motivates giving. Generosity arises from a heart of gratitude.

*Have you ever met an unhappy generous person? That's the reminder I see on a coffee cup that I got a few years back when Lea and I attended a conference offered by Generous Giving, a nonprofit whose mission is to spread the biblical message of generosity.* Through the years, I have witnessed many wealthy families experience deep satisfaction as they dedicate themselves to causes they care about. Some seem transformed, as if they have been set free from the bonds of materialism. Once they start giving—whether it's their money, time, or talents—they want to give more. Hearts grow stronger with exercise.

# Family Philanthropy

The old saying that "charity begins at home" is meant to warn against spending many hours and many dollars in service to strangers while neglecting one's own family. So true. The right balance is essential. Somehow, though, the saying also seems popular among people who feel reluctant to give anything at all to charity or others outside their family: *What, give away what we worked so hard to get? Our children come first!* One would hope that attitude carries through into showing up for their ball games instead of staying late for work.

Truth to tell, often the children already have quite enough—and, as we have seen, they may be worse off if they get too much. Even so, through smart financial planning and creative arrangements involving tax and insurance planning, many families manage to provide plenty to their favorite charitable causes and institutions without sacrificing their wealth. No need to get into those strategic details here. Such strategies have been around for generations, and other books and online resources spell it all out. My point is this: Philanthropy need not diminish how much the kids get. You can do more than you might think, and you should think about what matters most.

No matter how much money people have, however, they tend to worry that it won't be enough. The spirit of generosity seems unrelated to the degree of wealth. Some of the most dedicated givers have limited resources. In many cases, when clients begin a relationship with a wealth manager, the topic of charitable giving gets little attention. They say that they haven't thought much about it, or that they do not feel ready or rich enough, or that they fear it would shortchange the kids—and that's it. Case closed. The advisor interprets those comments as "not interested" and moves on to other important matters.

By contrast, I try to lead people into that conversation. As they explore the range of charitable options, they naturally get in touch with their values, which in turn draws families together, which in turn has a remarkable way of preserving and enhancing their wealth. Unity is essential for success. Family feuds destroy fortunes. So does family indifference. We must not forget those statistics showing that wealth often has nearly vanished after the third generation. Financial security is no guarantee of financial sustainability. The money does not vanish because it all goes to charity. It vanishes because the family cannot get its act together.

In other words, I agree that charity should begin at home—and by that, I mean that a family can find great strength in gathering, perhaps around the dinner table, to decide together who should benefit from the blessings that have come their way. They can make those decisions in the formal context of a private family foundation, or through the convenience of a donor advised fund (and again, there are countless resources explaining how to set those up). First though, they need to get started by sharing ideas with one another. The biggest step is to begin talking. Such conversations lead to a consensus of purpose. To put it simply: The family that gives together grows together. As mentioned in chapter 1, I've provided a "Discovering My Values" worksheet in Appendix A. With this, you can discover what matters most to your family to guide your decisions on philanthropy.

# Worthy to Contribute

More important than your net worth is your self-worth. When you believe in yourself, when you know that you stand on solid ground, you will not get lost in the shifting sands of other people's opinions. The prevailing culture of the world does not sway you. You can move forward boldly, sure of your decisions, without defining yourself by your failures.

Financial advisors who think holistically understand that a strong sense of self-worth is crucial to maintaining a thriving portfolio. Without that grounding, people tend to blow their money. Trying to make up for what is lacking inside, they search for other ways to demonstrate that they are valuable. They become self-absorbed and put on appearances, surrounding themselves with material possessions. They define themselves by what others think of them and how much influence they can wield. Anyone willing to listen will hear about their achievements and their status and the important people they know. Our culture encourages us to think that way. Ask a dozen people to tell you about themselves. Many will begin by describing what they do for a living. Their identity is their job.

Once people get in touch with a deeper set of values, they often find the contentment that had been so elusive. They finally can look outward rather than inward, and they discover that doing so does not hurt their livelihood. Instead, they are likely to thrive all the more and in a broader sense. They understand they are valuable not for what they do or whom they know but rather for who they are. Their newly found sense of self-worth opens their eyes to the worth in others and to a world of needs beyond themselves. Self-interest turns to social interest. They still want to be influential, but now, the emphasis is on things that matter to them. They aren't guessing what that might be. They are confident that they have something meaningful to contribute, and they know that they are worthy to serve others.

What they contribute is not limited to dollars. They can give not only their money but also their time and their voice. They can volunteer for causes that call for an army of dedicated souls, and they can speak out for those causes to persuade others to join in the effort. To give of one's time, in fact, can be a greater sacrifice. Money can be replaced. Time cannot. Time and advocacy do not require financial wealth, but they do require a wealth of dedication—and they are resources available to anyone. To give of oneself is not expensive, but it is costly.

## What Makes You Cry?

As I work with families who are considering philanthropy, I have often suggested that they ask themselves two questions. "How would you complete this sentence?" I ask. "Isn't it absurd that…." And the second question is simply this: "What makes you cry?"

Years ago, while attending a World Vision conference, my wife and I sat in on a talk by Gary Haugen, a human rights attorney who in 1997 founded International Justice Mission (IJM), a global network of volunteer lawyers who stand up for justice around the world. Haugen was speaking on the horrors of child trafficking in Southeast Asia. The organization has worked for the arrest of those who travel there to torment children. They face handcuffs the moment they step off the airplane to return to home soil.

Haugen showed us clips from a video that IJM made to see how far the traffickers would go. On the video, a "customer" wearing a hidden camera pretends to solicit services. The traffickers bring out a girl for his inspection. "Do you have something younger?" the man asks. They bring out another, and another, and each time he asks the same question. Haugen stopped the video. "For what they would pay back home to eat a simple meal," he said, "the customers can do whatever they want with these children."

Lea and I walked out of that room in tears, feeling utterly broken. "Those little girls," she said, "they're the same age as…"

"I know," I said and held her. "I know."

We resolved that we would join in the battle to eradicate that nightmare. Our family has since taken up child protection as a cause. That such iniquity persists—and it happens in America, too—is beyond absurd. Human trafficking, in all its manifestations, is evil. Having recognized it, it became impossible to go back to building our comfortable lifestyle knowing innocent lives are being enslaved. It can be a challenge for families of capacity to enjoy a comfortable life while conscious of the world's absurdities. Yet maybe this is a healthy tension to recognize.

What moves people to tears moves them to action, and we have plenty to cry about. Absurdities abound. It's a crime, too, when children starve. And when women are treated like little more than disposable property. Isn't it absurd that a good education is out of reach for so many people who could offer so much? And that much of the world lacks decent medical care? Or safe water? The list is endless.

Those two simple questions reach deep into the soul to get to the heart of what we deeply care about—and to reveal where we might contribute our money, our time, our voice, or all three. We don't need to wait till we are wealthy before acting. Setting up a family foundation is a good move, but what matters more is that families have a foundation. Mom and Dad should show, by example, their fundamental values and their passion for a cause. Children need to see their parents' tears and know that their family cares about much more than gadgets and baubles. If the kids inherit compassion, they can keep up the good work in a world of woes. As their turn comes, they will take charge of the mission along with the money. A continuity of purpose will persist through the generations. That lack of continuity has doomed many businesses as the changing leadership loses touch with the founding purpose and the spirit of entrepreneurship. Through the years, the mission gets lost in the transitions. What is true for a business is true for a family: Success comes when all involved, from the very top all the way down through the ranks, do not merely exist but instead rally behind an enduring vision.

When you can define the absurdities of today, you can imagine the possibilities of tomorrow. For example, imagine a world where children keep their innocence and are viewed as priceless; or a world where poverty is eradicated; or a world where women are no longer treated as someone's property; or a world where everyone has access to healthcare, education, and clean water. The list of hopeful possibilities is endless because the absurdities and needs are endless.

Ask yourself: What do you care about? How will you use your voice? What will be your legacy? You probably can list ten people who would be sure to come to your funeral, the people who matter most in your life and who probably know what makes you laugh and what makes you cry. In a few generations, though, will anyone remember your name? Will anyone know what you stood for? Do you matter? Your legacy is sowing seeds to a garden you may never see.

# Finding Purpose beyond Wealth

In my junior year of college, I took a class in which I had to deliver a persuasive speech that would get my audience to do something. I couldn't decide on a topic. It was a Saturday afternoon, and time was ticking. Looking for a diversion, I began flipping through TV stations and saw a commercial showing starving children in Africa, their bellies extended from malnutrition. It was hard to look, but I felt compelled. "For twenty dollars a month," the voiceover informed me, "you can do something about it."

The commercial got my mind totally off my worries about giving a speech—and suddenly, I realized that I had my topic. I would persuade my audience to donate money to save the life of a child. That simple exercise brought me into awareness of a critical need, and as soon as I could get the money together, I began sponsoring children through organizations like World Vision that developed a model that enables donors to support children living in extreme poverty.

In those days, millions had been orphaned by the HIV/AIDS pandemic. Scripture tells us that true religion calls us to care for widows and orphans in their distress. How might I help? As a finance student, I did the math, and the sheer numbers from the pandemic discouraged me. I heard estimates that about eleven million children in Africa had lost one or more parents and were in desperate need of help. How could I hope to make a difference? Then, it occurred to me that the U.S. population at the time was 240 million. *There's more of us than them*, I thought, *so if we just turned our hearts toward those orphaned children, the problem would be solved.* I knew I couldn't do it alone, but I saw the power of what we might accomplish collectively.

Why, I wondered, weren't more people doing something about such needs? Either they didn't know, or it was easier not to think about it. Like me, they had been changing channels looking for diversions. Such problems are so big that they can feel overwhelming: *How could one person possibly make a difference?* But that's where it starts. I'm reminded of the tale of the boy and the starfish. An old man is strolling on a vast beach littered with starfish after a storm. He encounters a boy who is busily picking them up, one at a time, and throwing them into the sea. "The starfish will die in the sun unless I put them back," the boy explains.

"Child, there must be tens of thousands of starfish on this beach," the old man tells him. "I'm afraid you won't be able to make much of a difference."

The boy bent down, picked up another starfish, and threw it as far as he could into the surf. Then, he turned to the old man and smiled. "It made a difference to that one!"

As a wealth manager, I serve people of means to help them grow their fortunes. I deal with their concerns and do my best to take good care of them. The better I do for them, the more I gain for our business. But I see another world, one of suffering people, longing for someone to advocate on their behalf, to provide support and care. I believe each of us has the capacity to fulfill this need, using our time, voices, and any resources we can gather, in various ways.

The irony is that I am a money man who sometimes finds himself telling people who have plenty that it's time to consider giving some of it away. I recognize and respect the power of money, but I know this, too, to be true: It must not come first. We must assign a purpose to money, and that purpose needs to be a force for good. I come back, time and again, to St. Paul's warning that the rich must not be arrogant and must put their hope in God, not in their uncertain wealth. Their duty, he wrote, is "to do good, to be rich in good deeds, and to be generous and willing to share" (Timothy 6:18 NIV).

How much is enough? We have been examining that question from various angles in this book, and here is another: If you have reached the point where another dollar, or another million of them, will do nothing to improve your life, consider how that money might improve the lives of others less fortunate than you. To you, it is excess. To them, it would be the difference between despair and hope, life and death.

You know you have enough when you discover everything you ever wanted is everything you already have. Those I have met who have discovered this reality are some of the most content, generous, and joyful people I know. So I'll ask again, Have you ever met an unhappy generous person?

# CHAPTER 7

# Everyone Is Included

---

"Would it be okay to take a vacation this year?" Jackie asked me. A longtime client, she had depended on her husband to decide such matters. Now, a widow for fifteen years, she was still in the pattern of asking permission. My wealth management firm had become sort of her surrogate husband for financial decisions.

Jackie certainly had the ability to decide for herself what she could afford, and frankly, she had been financially secure for years. Her husband, Paul, had done well in his accounting business and provided well for the family, but he was diagnosed with leukemia while only in his forties. Though Jackie also was well educated, she had decided to take on the full-time role of caring for their three children. He provided the income and managed the family finances. She managed the household. The family was thriving under that traditional arrangement. This was teamwork, and it all seemed so efficient.

The children had their mom at home with them, and Paul was able to focus on advancing his career and building for the family's future.

They never imagined that Paul would not share in that future. The cancer diagnosis shook their world. For five years, they hoped for the best, with much of their attention focused on Paul's struggle to regain his health. When he passed, Jackie felt lost. Not only was she dealing with her grief and trying to help the kids adjust to the loss of their dad, but the couple had not yet transitioned their financial affairs into Jackie's hands. Paul had done the basics of financial and estate planning, but the two of them never sat down to examine all the what-ifs.

Jackie was not lacking for money, though she was not sure of that. What she lacked was confidence and experience. Her college degree was in English literature, but she had put her career aspirations on hold. She had never felt inclined to deal with finances. She was good at math, but that wasn't her thing. That was Paul's thing.

Jackie turned to us for help, and I am pleased to report that she is doing well today. We were able to restore her confidence. Her children got a good education, and Jackie is enjoying life. She has gone on many vacations, and she also knows that the money will be sufficient to give the children a significant inheritance, although she has been considering how much is "enough." She wants to do right by them.

# A Tough Transition

The statistics bear out the fact that typically the husband dies before the wife. Often, she is left without the financial skills for effective money management. Besides the fact that women have a longer life span on average, our social norms have long suggested that handling the money is a man's job. In no way do I intend that to sound sexist.

It is simply an attitude still common in our culture, and I have seen both men and women subscribe to it.

As family models evolve, that is changing. No longer is it unusual for women to rise to the upper ranks of their careers while their husbands take the supportive role of maintaining the household and caring for the children. Among our clients, however, that arrangement is not typical. Many are from the baby boom generation or widows from the silent generation, where traditional roles still predominate. These are one-earner households where the man makes and manages the money. The woman defers to his financial decisions, while he defers to her domestic decisions. With so much to do, they see it as teamwork. They are delegating the duties.

It's not uncommon for couples to have that divide-and-conquer mentality. For some, it works, yet the risk is that the wives may eventually become widows who do not know how to handle money. In my three decades of practice, I have seen that often. The women come to us puzzled, sometimes overwhelmed, and often worried. We can set them on the right course, but it would have been far better had they been following that course with their husbands all along. Money management should not be unilateral. Making decisions jointly is healthier and promotes spousal unity. Pardon the cliché, but two heads are better than one. Each might see something that the other missed. Both should be informed and able to make educated decisions so that neither is left vulnerable if the other passes away. Business partners prepare for such a situation. So should life partners.

Sometimes, the surviving spouse never does make the transition to becoming an effective money manager. I have known widows who, thirty years after their husband died, still called their financial advisor asking permission to take a vacation or buy a car or some other expense. More often than not, they easily can afford it. They are looking for a surrogate voice of reassurance, and we are happy to fill that role. Meanwhile, we strive to build their self-confidence. Some get to the point where they feel secure making financial decisions. Others will want affirmation till their dying day.

Feelings of guilt also can linger long after a loved one's passing—as was the case with my client Jackie, who still felt uncomfortable fifteen years later about having fun without Paul at her side. My father knows that feeling. He and Mom had long dreamed of visiting Jerusalem and the Holy Land, and in 2018, they finally booked a cruise there. They were excited at the prospect of traveling with a group of friends to see the historical sites that mark the birth of their faith.

Then, Mom died, and Dad was heartbroken. "We were supposed to do this together," Dad kept saying. "How could I ever go alone?"

Another gentleman who had booked the trip approached him. "My wife died years ago," he told my dad, "but I remember that feeling. You were so looking forward to sharing this with her." He smiled gently. "You know, I'm traveling there as a single guy, too. Why don't you come anyway, and you and I can share a cabin?" Dad agreed, and the two of them had a great time together—although his pangs of guilt reminded him how much he would have loved for Mom to be there by his side.

I would rather think of those pangs as reminders of love. I can say with assurance that missing out on life was not what Paul would have wanted for Jackie, and that's not what Mom would want for Dad, either.

## On the Same Page

If you look around the room at a major financial conference, you will see that most of the attendees are men. I have been to events that draw thousands of investment professionals from around the country and the world, and the great majority are men. Most of the college students studying finance or accounting or economics are men. Most financial advisors are men. It's getting better, although still today men outnumber women in the financial services industry.

Some would say it's nature and some would say it's nurture, but for whatever reason women do not focus as much as men on money. Perhaps the long-standing perception that the man should be the provider and protector plays a part. Parents lead their children, not necessarily consciously, onto the path in life that they believe is most appropriate for boys and for girls. Even in our changing society, gender roles persist.

Certainly there is no difference in male and female brain power, as has been demonstrated time and time again. Women are equally able to deal with numbers. Heart power is a different matter. Our culture has long encouraged women to develop their nurturing nature. Men, too, have plenty of heart power, but our culture tends to downplay it. Little girls get dolls. Little boys get toy soldiers.

I point this out because women, who typically live longer than their husbands, frequently are left holding the purse strings of the family finances. Wise money management is a product of education, experience, and temperament. Women can quickly learn whatever they do not already know, gaining further insights along the way, and those who have managed households and raised children have a valuable perspective on matters that need to be included in the conversation.

As noted earlier, trillions will pass to the next generation but not before it transfers to the hands of Mom's control. She will decide how it will be used and who stewards the balance when she is gone. Melinda French Gates resigned from the Bill and Melinda Gates Foundation and the foundation name will now be known as the Gates Foundation. She parts with $12.5 billion dedicated her philanthropic work for women rights and inequality issues. Most women will control a far more modest measure of wealth—but multiply that by millions of families, and the sum is staggering.

Also huge is the potential for that money to improve lives in countless ways if it is managed wisely. All those women who for years poured out love to their families are likely, as a whole, to direct the money where they believe it will do the most good. That does not necessarily mean that it will go to the kids. As experienced moms, they tend to know what is good for their children and what could hurt them. They watched out for them, disciplined them, dried their tears, cheered them on, and launched them into life. Certainly, the moms do not begrudge the kids a share of the family wealth, but they are not about to bury them under a mountain of money. They want the next generation to grow up strong, and that means first helping those who are truly in need.

This is not to say that men are out of touch and don't care, but in traditional household, the dad is away at work much of the time and it is Mom who deals with the skinned knees. Even when both parents are employed, as is often the case, Mom still tends to be the one who knows the names of the children's friends and teachers. She is tuned in to her children's personalities and preferences. She understands the everyday dynamics of family life, and those dynamics have everything to do with success.

Family dysfunction destroys fortunes. The wife's insights can forestall such a sad outcome. Sometimes, though, the dysfunction effectively rules her out. Her husband might take the attitude of *I earned it, so I call the shots,* leaving her in the dark about how he is managing the money, if he is managing it at all. Or he might withhold or lavish money to get his way. He tries to control her behavior through punishment and reward. That might be a good way to train a puppy, but it can kill the spirit of unity that is essential in a healthy marriage. Getting things done requires cooperation, not manipulation.

With such marital issues getting in the way, it's little wonder that so many women become disenfranchised. Whether the husband dies or the marriage ends in divorce, the woman finds herself beginning over but lacking essential financial skills. I have worked with many widows and divorcees as they try to put their lives back together after abusive relationships. Typically, they feel isolated and lack confidence. First on the agenda is reassuring them that they have what it takes to succeed.

Marital unity is essential for healthy family life. Husband and wife must each bring their strengths to the table and make the most of them. If Mom and Dad are not on the same page, the kids will see that soon enough. To get what they want, the kids will find the path of least resistance, playing their parents off each other. Family meetings are a good place to demonstrate unity to the kids—but you can only demonstrate what you already possess. If it's just a show, the kids will see that, too.

Husband and wife are individuals, of course, who will differ in their talents and interests and predispositions. Neither should get lost in the other, but they should stand strong together in their resolve to pursue family values, which they must be able to clearly articulate. They must talk openly and often. Sharing is caring.

In marriage, "the two shall become one," the Scriptures tell us. "This is a great mystery"—and it is also a concept of great beauty with the power to strengthen families immensely. It is also one of the greatest struggles in marriage because the tension lies between which one to become: more like him or more like her? I submit that oneness looks more like unity in uniqueness. No one is perfect, so when two imperfect people are joined together, the result will not be a perfect relationship. Family unity will require a lot of work, good communication, and above all, grace.

# The WOW Factor

Several years ago, when it became clear that we had a growing clientele of women, many of them widowed or divorced, we resolved to find an avenue for them to gather and ask questions and learn. We created a service at Apriem called WOW, or Women of Wisdom. WOW is a series of educational events designed to encourage and empower women on personal finances and life issues. Our company president, Rhonda, chooses the speakers and introduces them, working with the other women on our staff who handle the logistics of organizing the events. It's a program run by women for the benefit of women.

For our first event, which we held at a nice steakhouse, we sent out invitations to our women clients and to the wives of our male clients. If a husband and wife both were clients, only the woman got an invitation. We planned a welcoming session at which we also would give them an economic update. Soon after the invitations went out, several calls came in, all with the same question: "May my husband attend, too? He's really interested in hearing what you all have to say." It seemed like a reasonable request.

More than seventy people attended, including quite a few men. Afterward, we congratulated ourselves, feeling that the inaugural session had been a flying success. I had noticed, though, that during the Q and A session after the presentation, most of the questions came from the men, not from the women.

Back at the office the next day, I got a call from a longtime client, Naomi, a woman who always has given me honest and helpful feedback. I had seen her sitting at the back of the room during the presentation. "Great event, Harmon," she said, "but do you want to hear my thoughts?"

"Always."

"Okay, look, if you really want these events to encourage and empower women, you need to create a safe place for them. With their husbands there, they don't have that," she said. "From where I was sitting, I could see everything that was going on. I saw one woman raise her hand to ask a question, but she put it back down after her husband whispered something to her. Then he raised *his* hand. She never got a chance to ask her question, but he sure did—or rather, he made his statement. He was that guy who was talking about foreign currency and stuff that I don't understand and don't want to understand."

"Yeah, I remember him," I said. "He seemed like he wanted to run the show." It's not unusual for men to seem more interested in displaying what they know rather than listening and learning. I call it intellectual testosterone.

"Didn't you notice, Harmon, that the men kind of took over when it was question time? This was an event that was meant for women, but the women seemed to be shutting down—because they could tell that it wasn't really about them. I can't see how this is going to work unless the men simply aren't invited."

I had no doubt that she was right. When we sent the invitations for our next WOW event, we made it clear that this was for women only and that they should not bring their husbands. A few of those husbands called me to ask why, and I explained that sometimes it's best when women talk with other women. Sometimes, the men joke with me about it: "So when are you going to have a MOW event, for men of wisdom? How about a fishing trip or something, just for us guys?" The truth is, men generally don't need empowerment. Society has already given them more than their fair share.

As long as the women keep attending, we will keep offering this program. If they stop coming, we will know that they have heard all they need to hear. No sign of that yet. The events are still popular, and I find it interesting that the ones with the greatest attendance are on non-financial topics. We include talks on health and wellness and other quality of life issues. When a doctor gave a presentation about the relationship between sleep and good physical and mental health, we had to set up chairs in a back room of the restaurant to accommodate the crowd. You might think a topic such as that has little to do with personal finance. In truth, it has everything to do with it. Lack of sleep breeds anxiety and distorts judgment. If you are sleep deprived, you won't make the best decisions on money matters.

Apriem Advisors is committed to including women powerfully in the conversation—single or married, divorced or widowed, wherever they might be in life. It's not really a conversation at all if the women do not participate. Their brain and heart power are indispensable. They tend to be particularly tuned in to the relationships and values and family dynamics that must be addressed for real success. They see things that men might overlook, and what they see often is what matters most.

# Investment in Togetherness

"I want to put a pizza oven in the backyard," my wife told me one evening.

"Huh?"

"A wood-burning pizza oven," Lea said, parting the curtain to point out the window. "It can go right over there." I could see in her eyes that she was envisioning the thing already fired up. We had been talking about redesigning our outdoor areas, but this was news to me.

"Domino's pizza delivery is good enough, though," I said. "I mean, we can always..." I needed time to think this through. Claiming that Domino's was good wasn't exactly a strong argument, but it seemed better than suggesting some frozen brand from the supermarket.

"No, no, no, this will be fun!" she said. "It will be good for our family. You'll see." Lea did some research and found a contractor who could get us an imported Italian brick oven for thousands of dollars installed. As usual, I did the math. We could buy hundreds of pizzas from the nearest pizza franchise for significantly less money.

Turns out it wasn't about the math at all. It was about the memories. That brick oven has become a highlight of our social life. We gather around it when people visit, and our kids invite their friends for pizza parties. And I must say, pizza doesn't get better than what comes out of that wood-burning pizza oven.

My point is that Lea was right, and for all my talk about the things in life that matter most, I had tried to reduce her vision to dollars and cents. I was looking at the bottom line. My wife was looking at the possibilities. She could see what I didn't, which was an opportunity to further strengthen our family bonds with a special place to talk and laugh and enjoy life. We weren't buying an extravagance. We were investing in togetherness.

I am convinced that women and men perceive the world from different lenses. For example, from the type of questions asked during a couple's initial consultation with a financial advisor, the men ask a lot of quantitative questions: *What is your performance record? Where do you think the markets are heading? Will interest rates be rising?* They gather facts. They want data. Their decision on whether to hire the advisor is based on the bottom line. Women care about that information too, but they tend to go with a gut feeling. "I liked him," a wife might tell her husband afterward. "I think that meeting went well."

Or: "Sure, he knows his stuff, but can we trust him?" She understands the data, but her assessment is not only quantitative but also qualitative. It is also based on a feeling—how she feels during and after the meeting. And if she has a bad feeling, she will not want to proceed.

A lot of financial advisors, convinced that the husband makes all the decisions, scarcely acknowledge the wife when meeting with a couple. After a polite hello, they don't look at her or ask her to weigh in on the discussion. Yes, many wives do defer to the husband's leadership, and some let him do all the talking, but that doesn't render a woman invisible. In fact, a caring husband often defers to his wife, in the spirit of marital unity—"the two shall become one." He is slow to speak and quick to listen.

Financial advisors, too, would do well to do a lot more listening. They should draw out the woman's voice and encourage equal participation because a wife and mother likely has a perspective that is aligned with what is best for the family. She sees what her husband, so busy collecting facts, might not see. Our standard practice at Apriem is to engage both spouses during the initial meeting and at the subsequent reviews. An advisor who professes to care about family finance should never tune out the one who is likely the most tuned in.

# The Power of Teamwork

My grandmother Eunice Kong, or "Tai Tai" as we called her, was born and raised in Hawaii and embraced a "live and let live" philosophy of acceptance, in keeping with the island culture. Though she stood by her values, she never voiced much disapproval of other's opinions and attitudes. "To each his own," she simply would say, by which she meant that she would not judge those whose views differed from hers. She would allow them the dignity to conduct their lives as they saw fit.

As I regard some of the challenges and divisiveness in this world, I shake my head and tell myself that I might be happier taking Grandma's hands-off approach toward our fellow travelers. As a financial planner, however, I know that our clients instead want a helping hand—and that is the spirit of Ohana, which also runs deep in Hawaiian culture.

# The Pieces of the Puzzle

Throughout every chapter of this book, in one way or another, I have emphasized the importance of the relational aspects of wealth management. We've explored the risks of passing on wealth to heirs without adequate preparation and the importance of open dialogue within families about money, purpose, and legacy. We've discussed the importance of clarifying family core values before addressing the practical details of investment and estate planning. Your wealth has immense power, and it's important to support the matters that mean most to your family.

Remember, money alone does not bring happiness or security—it is the deeper relationships, shared purpose, and commitment to one another that truly matter. We've learned how dysfunctional family dynamics can undermine responsible financial management. And I shared how my own family uses meetings to discuss values, goals, and plans so we can ensure we use our resources to make a positive impact. I encourage you to do the same, and I've included resources in the Appendix sections to help guide you. The ultimate aim is to cultivate financial freedom grounded in security, peace of mind, and purpose.

Exploring this further, we learned how one can find purpose beyond the accumulation of wealth. Rather than defining success by material wealth, we should place greater value on the impact we have on our family and others. By using family meetings, you can openly discuss financial matters at home with your children. This will foster unity and could help avoid conflict later. This also gives you the opportunity to educate your children on the difference between equality and fairness when making financial decisions.

Finally, we learned of the challenges faced by women when it comes to family finances. Widowed women are often not informed on financial matters, leaving many unprepared when the family's wealth is passed on. This is something we've made great effort to correct at Apriem. After all, Mom will often be there first before the kids get their hands on the family treasures. I encourage families of all kinds to communicate openly about their finances. Even if one spouse won't be playing an active role in asset management, their unique perspective and values should be taken into account when making financial decisions.

# Life Is a Team Sport

At some point in life, most of us come to realize that we can't go it alone. We need partners. We need others on whom we can depend and who will hold us accountable. Your own efforts cannot get you all the way. It's simple, really: If you are not the expert, align yourself with somebody who is. That person, in turn, very well might need your brand of expertise. It's also been said, if you want to go fast, go alone, but if you want to go far, go together.

That symbiotic relationship is called teamwork, which is essential in the financial advisory industry if the client is to be served well. Collectively, the team members possess a powerful knowledge base, but it is useful only if they are communicating. That is where the wealth manager comes into play. Apriem facilitates the conversation. We know the needs, goals, and dreams of each of our clients, and our job is to ensure that everyone's efforts fit into a strategy for success.

I admire an independent spirit, so long as it does not mean having a closed mind that rejects what other good minds have to offer. There's no place for know-it-alls. Arrogance is financially perilous. It alienates and isolates. The financial world has become exceedingly complex, and those who think that they know it all are destined to be proved wrong. It is good to be confident, but it is never good to be cocksure.

People who believe that they cannot go wrong see no reason to plan for life's contingencies.

The consequences can be devastating to family wealth. On the Internet, you can readily find story after story about celebrities who, for lack of consultation and planning, blew it financially. The pattern is predictable: They live as if they expect never to die, which they do—and their estates dwindle away in contentious and protracted court cases. Blinded by their own material success, they might have thought that they did not need anyone's financial advice. No doubt their heirs, if there are any, feel differently.

Working cooperatively requires humility—and "with humility comes wisdom," the Proverbs tell us. First, you must concede that you need other people. Then, as you work together, you need to stay in your own lane, respecting the skills and talents that others possess and keeping out of their way so that they can do their job. For example, an accountant, unless specially qualified, should not be dispensing investment advice. Ditto for an attorney giving tax advice, or a wealth manager giving legal advice.

Life is a team sport. Even if you were the best athlete in the league, you could not hope to win the championship without all the players supporting one another. We must choose carefully the people with whom we want to play ball, and we must respect their positions in the field. The shortstop is there for a specific reason. So is the outfielder.

The extent of expert advice that a family requires will depend, of course, upon the complexities of that family's finances. Some families need to learn how to set up charitable foundations, while others need to learn how to set up monthly budgets. I have not written this book as a guide for the rich and famous. I have written it as a guide for any family that is accumulating money and wishes to do the right thing with it. Mistakes can cost a fortune—and the biggest ones often result from paying little attention to what matters most.

Ultimately, my hope is that you'll begin laying the groundwork to have these discussions within your own families. The work you do now will not only benefit your current family but also the generations to come. Money has immense power. It has the power to tear apart families if these topics are not openly discussed. But it also has the power to do good. If you want to ensure the best for your family for generations to come, I urge you to get started now. Schedule your first family meeting. Use the material in the appendix to discover the values that mean the most to your family and create a family mission statement. Above all, I encourage you to simply communicate openly as a family about money issues. I promise you won't regret it.

And remember what matters most—valuables are fleeting and temporary, but your family values truly have a lasting impact.

# Thank you for Reading
## *Values Over Valuables*

I am truly grateful that you've taken the time to read this book and explore how to build a life centered on your deepest values. I hope my experiences and insights have inspired you to reflect on what matters most to you and your loved ones.

My heart's desire is to see families thriving and making a difference in their communities and the world. Remember, this is just the beginning of your journey if you dare to take the next steps to live the life money can't buy. I'm here to walk alongside you as you put these principles into practice wishing greater purpose, unity, and joy for generations.

## Explore more *Values Over Valuables* Resources

The concepts in this book have the power to transform your relationships and your legacy—but only if you intentionally put them into practice. To support you in your journey, I've created some additional resources, including an exercise to identify your core values, discussion guides for family meetings, and tools for purposeful multigenerational wealth management.

# Let's Connect!

If I can ever be a resource to you, please don't hesitate to reach out. You can find me on LinkedIn at: https://www.linkedin.com/in/harmon-kong-54600b3/

To learn more about how my team at Apriem Advisors helps families manage wealth purposefully for generations, visit us at: www.Apriem.com.

# Making a Difference Together

If this book made a difference for you, I'd be so grateful if you shared it with others. Please consider writing an honest review on Amazon, Goodreads, or the platform of your choosing to help new readers feel confident selecting it. Your support allows this message to reach more people.

Until we connect again, I'm cheering you on!

Your friend,
Harmon

# Discovering My Values
# Worksheet

## INSTRUCTIONS:

Discovering your values can be a powerful tool for helping you identify your core values that drive your life vision and mission. It is the essence of who you are and what is most important to you. As you work through this process, it can be a source of discovery to what also matters most to your family.

1. **Select up to 10 words below that resonate with you.** If you are doing this with your spouse, complete this separately, then compare the values you selected. Discover the ones you have in common. An appropriate amount would be 5 to 7 core values that become your family's guiding principles.

| | | | |
|---|---|---|---|
| Accountability | Equality | Happiness | Patience |
| Authenticity | Fairness | Health | Peace |
| Balance | Faith | Honesty | Resilience |
| Community | Family | Humility | Respect |
| Compassion | Finances | Independence | Responsibility |
| Courage | Forgiveness | Innovation | Self-discipline |
| Creativity | Freedom | Integrity | Service |
| Curiosity | Friendship | Justice | Sports |
| Determination | Fun | Kindness | Success |
| Education | Generosity | Love | Tolerance |
| Empathy | Gratitude | Loyalty | Trust |
| Environmentalism | Growth | Open-mindedness | Unity |

Write your own values: _____ _____ _____

2. For each value you selected, expand on your choice and discuss why they are important and write them down for clarity.

**For example:**

**Family** is important to us because maintaining strong relationships with our family members and spending quality time with them is how we build unity and love for each other.

**Education** is important to us because we believe in continuous learning leads to personal growth and enrichment in our life.

**Humility** is important to us because it fosters positive interpersonal relationships. When we are humble, we are more likely to listen to others, acknowledge our mistakes, and show respect and empathy toward others. This can lead to healthier and more harmonious interactions with friends, family, colleagues, and even strangers.

Name: _____

# Discovering My Values Worksheet

## 10 WORDS THAT RESONATE WITH ME:

| | |
|---|---|
| 1. | 6. |
| 2. | 7. |
| 3. | 8. |
| 4. | 9. |
| 5. | 10. |

## WHY THESE WORDS ARE IMPORTANT TO ME:

| | |
|---|---|
| 1. | |
| 2. | |
| 3. | |

| | |
|---|---|
| 4. | |
| 5. | |
| 6. | |
| 7. | |
| 8. | |
| 9. | |
| 10. | |

# Our Family's Guiding Principles

After separately completing the "Discovering My Values Worksheet," discover the ones you have in common with your family members. An appropriate amount would be 5 to 7 core values that become your family's guiding principles.

## OUR FAMILY CORE VALUES:

| | |
|---|---|
| 1. | 5. |
| 2. | 6. |
| 3. | 7. |
| 4. | |

## WHY THESE VALUES ARE IMPORTANT TO OUR FAMILY:

| | |
|---|---|
| 1. | |
| 2. | |
| 3. | |

| | |
|---|---|
| 4. | |
| 5. | |
| 6. | |
| 7. | |

# Sample Family Vision and Mission Statements

## Values of Education, Hard Work, Family, Community, and Generosity

### FAMILY VISION STATEMENT:

We envision a family where education is valued as the cornerstone of personal growth, where hard work is celebrated as the pathway to success, where bonds of family strengthen our unity, where community involvement enriches our lives, and where generosity toward others defines our legacy.

### FAMILY MISSION STATEMENT:

Our family is committed to fostering an environment where learning is embraced, where each member strives for excellence through hard work, where we prioritize quality time together to nurture our familial bonds, where we actively engage with and contribute to our local community, and where acts of generosity toward others are woven into the fabric of our daily lives.

## FAMILY VISION STATEMENT:

In our family, education is treasured as the key to unlocking endless opportunities, hard work is revered as the foundation of achievement, family bonds are cherished as the source of our strength, community involvement is valued as our responsibility, and generosity toward others is our guiding principle.

## FAMILY MISSION STATEMENT:

Our mission as a family is to prioritize education by fostering a culture of curiosity and lifelong learning, to instill a strong work ethic in each member by leading by example, to nurture our familial connections through open communication and shared experiences, to actively participate in our community to make a positive impact, and to practice generosity by giving back and supporting those in need.

## FAMILY VISION STATEMENT:

As a family, we aspire to create a legacy where education empowers us, hard work propels us, family ties bind us, community engagement enriches us, and generosity defines us.

## FAMILY MISSION STATEMENT:

Our family is dedicated to promoting education by encouraging intellectual curiosity and continuous learning, to embodying the value of hard work through perseverance and dedication to our goals, to nurturing our familial relationships through love, support, and respect, to actively participating in our community to promote positive change, and to embracing generosity by sharing our blessings with others in need.

# Kong Family Values: Community, Faith, Family, Generosity, and Service

## FAMILY VISION STATEMENT:

Our family envisions a world where community thrives, faith guides our actions, family bonds are unbreakable, generosity flows freely, and service is our legacy.

## FAMILY MISSION STATEMENT:

As a family, we are committed to nurturing a vibrant community where we support and uplift one another, to living out our faith through love, compassion, and integrity in all that we do, to prioritizing quality time together to strengthen our familial connections, to embracing a spirit of generosity by sharing our resources and talents with those in need, and to serving others with humility and empathy to make a positive impact on the world.

## FAMILY VISION STATEMENT:

As a family, we envision a future where community unity thrives, faith serves as our compass, family ties remain unbreakable, generosity knows no bounds, and service to others is our highest calling.

## FAMILY MISSION STATEMENT:

Our family is dedicated to building strong ties within our community through active participation and support, to living out our faith by embodying its principles of love, forgiveness, and compassion, to nurturing our family relationships through shared experiences and unwavering support, to embracing a culture of generosity by giving freely of our time, resources, and talents, and to serving others with humility and empathy to create a more just and compassionate world.

# Family Values of Faith, Family, Fitness, Finances, and Fun

### FAMILY VISION STATEMENT:

Our family envisions a life where faith strengthens our bonds, family is our foundation, fitness promotes vitality, finances provide stability, and fun brings joy to our journey.

### FAMILY MISSION STATEMENT:

As a family, we are committed to deepening our faith through shared spiritual practices and mutual support, to prioritizing quality time together to nurture our familial connections, to promoting physical well-being through regular exercise and healthy lifestyle choices, to managing our finances responsibly to secure our future and support our goals, and to embracing opportunities for laughter, adventure, and relaxation to create lasting memories and foster a sense of joy in our lives.

### FAMILY VISION STATEMENT:

In our family, we aspire to integrate faith into every aspect of our lives, to prioritize our familial relationships above all else, to maintain physical fitness for overall well-being, to manage our finances wisely for financial security and abundance, and to infuse every day with moments of fun and laughter.

## FAMILY MISSION STATEMENT:

Our family's mission is to deepen our faith through prayer, reflection, and service to others, to strengthen our family bonds through open communication, love, and support, to prioritize physical fitness through regular exercise and healthy habits, to manage our finances with diligence, planning, and generosity, and to intentionally seek out opportunities for fun, relaxation, and shared experiences that bring us closer together.

## FAMILY VISION STATEMENT:

As a family, we envision a life where faith guides our decisions, family is our greatest treasure, fitness empowers our bodies and minds, finances provide stability and abundance, and fun enriches our everyday experiences.

## FAMILY MISSION STATEMENT:

Our family is dedicated to deepening our faith through prayer, worship, and service to others, to nurturing our family relationships through communication, love, and support, to prioritizing physical fitness through regular exercise, healthy eating, and self-care practices, to managing our finances responsibly through budgeting, saving, and investing for the future, and to embracing opportunities for fun, adventure, and laughter to create cherished memories together.

# Family Goal Sheet

Name: _____ Date: _____

## LOVE LANGUAGE:

| Words of Affirmation | Physical Touch | Gifts | Quality Time | Acts of Service |
|:---:|:---:|:---:|:---:|:---:|
| ☐ | ☐ | ☐ | ☐ | ☐ |

## GOALS:

1. _____

2. _____

3. _____

## STRENGTHS:

1. _____

2. _____

3. _____

## WEAKNESSES:

1. _____

2. _____

3. _____

## PRAYERS:

1. _____

2. _____

3. _____

## ANSWERED PRAYERS:

1. _____

2. _____

3. _____

## SPIRITUAL:

1. _____

2. _____

3. _____

## MINISTRY:

1. _____

2. _____

3. _____

# SCHOOL:

1. _____

2. _____

3. _____

# ACTIVITIES:

1. _____

2. _____

3. _____

# SOCIAL/FRIENDS:

1. _____

2. _____

3. _____

# OTHERS:

1. _____

2. _____

3. _____

# Kong Ohana House Rules

I acknowledge that I am not perfect, yet I understand that I have the free will to make good choices and bad choices. As a result, I have the power to influence good or bad consequences; therefore I take full responsibility for every thought, word, and action in my life. I am committed to the following family expectations:

1. I will treat others as I want to be treated.
2. I will do the best I can in everything and not quit, complain, or criticize.
3. I will think positively and use positive words when speaking to others. No name-calling or teasing each other or people outside our family.
4. I will strive to work together as a family knowing that we are always better when we are together.
5. I will not tell lies but rather always tell the truth in love, no matter how difficult.
6. I will demonstrate compassion toward others, especially when the other is hurt or not feeling well.
7. (Children) I will honor and obey my parents, trusting that they know what is best for me.

8. (Mom) I will be my children's greatest fan by encouraging them to achieve their highest God-given potential. I will support my husband with all my heart.

9. (Dad) I will lead my family by example, following God's calling for a husband and father: to love, protect, and provide for my wife and children.

10. I have been blessed and I will be thankful and strive to be a blessing to others whenever, wherever, and however possible.

*February 24, 2008*
*Family Meeting*